Catching the Writing Express

—

Lessons from the South Bay Writing Project

Grades 2–4

by Iris M. Tiedt and Lisa Johnson

Fearon Teacher Aids
a division of
David S. Lake Publishers
Belmont, California 94002

Lesson plans are based on the contributions of the following teachers:

Clark R. Barton

Pauline J. Blissett

Anne Carlson

Sandra J. Hall

Geraldine Mulford

Kelly C. Noftz

Rose Marie Ranada

J. Saxten-Sallen

Ann Stekelberg

Judy Wilcher

Cover and book illustrator: Duane Bibby

Entire contents copyright © 1987 by David S. Lake Publishers, 19 Davis Drive, Belmont, California 94002. Permission is hereby granted to reproduce designated materials in this book for noncommercial classroom and individual use.

ISBN 0-8224-1307-8

Printed in the United States of America

1. 9 8 7 6 5 4 3 2 1

Contents

Kids Can Write!

Children prepare to write as they begin to learn language. As toddlers—even as infants—they already listen to language around them, and their active brains absorb the sounds of language. Soon they try to make meaningful sounds themselves. Gradually they make sounds they learn to associate with certain meanings—for example, "ma-ma" and "da-da." We respond encouragingly, and the child talks and talks and talks!

Most children are self-motivated to learn language. They listen and practice during all their waking hours. Without instruction, they observe how the system of language works. They notice patterns, the way words go together to make sense.

The two-year-old creates brief but meaningful sentences: "Daddy up. Johnny go. All gone truck." But this child grammar evolves as the child gains a greater understanding of grammar. The four-year-old's sentences are fuller than the two-year-old's: "Give me the ball, Meggie, or I'll tell Mommy." By the time children enter kindergarten, they are chattering fluently, using a wide range of grammatical structures.

Children compose sentences all the time, running them freely through their "grammar machines" so the sentences make sense to them. The eight-year-old's sentences are quite complex: "Hey, Tom, ask your dad if you can come over to my house after school tomorrow." Tom immediately decodes the sentence, runs to ask his dad, and is back to report, "Yeah, Kurt, he says it will be okay as long as I come home in time for supper." The children may not know the terms of grammar—nouns, verbs, adjectives, dependent clauses, or compound sentences. But they intuitively apply complex rules of grammar as they compose a variety of sentences during conversation.

Oral language experiences prepare children to write. Children draw on their knowledge of words and concepts, such as the ideas they remember from books read aloud to them, or concepts they have talked about with friends or family. Stored in their brains is a wealth of knowledge that we will help them tap as they begin to write.

We of the South Bay Writing Project have written this book to help you:

- Use oral language to support writing
- Build children's self-esteem through writing
- Guide students to write successfully
- Make use of reading and writing connections
- Show young writers how to improve their writing

The writing lessons in this book are grouped into seven units, arranged sequentially to complement the development of writing skills. Each unit contains from three to six separate writing lessons. These writing lessons have been developed and written by teachers, the same teachers who use these lessons in their own classrooms.

A lesson plan directed to the teacher introduces each writing lesson. In most cases, a reproducible page used for that lesson and directed to the student follows the lesson plan page. The lesson plan format may be adapted to numerous other writing activities of your own design. Using the lessons in this book will help you plan writing lessons of your own that both you and your students will enjoy, lessons that will help them grow as writers.

About the South Bay Writing Project

The South Bay Writing Project was created in 1976 as part of the California Writing Project and the National Writing Project. The organization is located at San Jose State University in San Jose, California. It serves students, teachers, and schools in the southern portion of the Bay Area.

The South Bay Writing Project follows the two major thrusts of the writing project model: a summer writing institute that trains K–14 teacher consultants, and ongoing staff development for local teachers. In addition, the project has innovated other activities designed to stimulate and to improve student writing, such as the Young Writers' Conference and a Computers in Language Arts Conference.

Through our work with the South Bay Writing Project, we are always learning more about how to teach writing. We want to share some of these principles with you.

Writing is thinking

Thinking and expressing thoughts develop together from the time of a child's birth. As children become aware of written language, they are motivated to express their ideas in writing. Their writing reveals what they are thinking about. Putting thoughts in writing helps children clarify and organize their thinking.

Oral language provides the foundation for writing

Children develop oral language before they work with written language. This prior knowledge of vocabulary and ideas is essential to successful writing. We need to expose children to concepts and experiences so they have something to say, and the tools with which to say it before we ask them to write.

Children learn to write by reading

Through listening to stories and reading what others write, children develop a sense of story or a sense of how others make a statement. By observing the writing of skilled authors, students learn ways to improve their own writing. Improving writing is a matter of grammar and style.

Children learn to write by writing

In order to learn to write with ease, children need to write frequently. They can write lists, notes, questions, answers to questions, conversations, paragraphs, memories, stories, reports, poems, and so on. They will benefit from writing on a daily basis.

We can teach young writers to improve their writing abilities

The ability to write well comes from practice, persistence, and the discovery that writing is enjoyable. We can help students find this joy by making them feel comfortable with writing, comfortable enough to practice and persevere. We must start by accepting the beginning writers' early efforts, praising students for what they have achieved. By talking about writing and by observing the writing of others, young writers will learn how to make their writing more effective. We can guide them to experiment with new styles, new forms, and more sophisticated ways of writing.

This book contains writing lessons that will help you teach writing based on these principles. You can also create writing lessons of your own using interesting ideas that you already have. The rest of this introduction shows you how to create lessons that engage students in the writing process.

The best writing lesson begins with objectives. Think about what you want your students to learn during the course of that lesson. Your objectives should be specific, but they may also be flexible.

Objectives may reflect what you expect students to demonstrate during the lesson. Or they may tell what you expect students to be able to accomplish as a result of the lesson. Objectives may also describe what skills the lesson allows students to practice. Here are some examples of objectives.

Students will:
1. Discuss a controversial issue and express an opinion.
2. Recognize adjectives.
3. Write an expository paragraph.
4. Tell a story about a real event.
5. Use transitions as they relate a sequence of events.
6. Identify the point of view in a story.
7. Proofread other students' stories.
8. Suggest ways to improve a composition.

A lesson plan usually has a few related objectives. When you write your own lessons, you will want to create a plan that incorporates the objectives you have selected. List your objectives and keep them in mind during the lesson.

Each lesson plan in this book has four essential components: the **s**timulus (or prewriting activity), the main **a**ctivity, the **f**ollow-up activity, and the **e**valuation. The key words of this plan form the acronym "SAFE." Let's take a look at each component of the SAFE Lesson Plan.

Stimulus

Any part of the lesson that occurs before students write, and that is intended to stimulate writing, may be considered the stimulus. Listening to a story read aloud often stimulates writing. Other stimulus activities include watching a film, observing an unusual object, and participating in a field trip. The stimulus activities in this book almost always include group discussion and preparation for the main activity.

Activity

The main activity is the performance by the students. Usually this performance will be a form of writing. Occasionally the activity may be oral, designed to parallel the writing program.

Students may write (or present orally) paragraphs, stories, reports, letters, poems, skits, dialogues, essays, and so on. They may perform skits or role-play situations they envision. In short, the lessons in this book cover a wide variety of forms as main activities.

Follow-up

The follow-up activity is defined as whatever occurs after the main activity. It should be designed to support the main activity. Usually the follow-up will be a postwriting activity.

Postwriting activities are highly motivating and encourage further writing, so they are important to the success of a particular lesson. The postwriting activities in this book usually involve students sharing their stories or compositions, editing or correcting surface errors, rewriting, or completing stories begun.

Evaluation

Teachers are encouraged to use a variety of techniques to evaluate students' writing. Sometimes it is more appropriate for students to evaluate each other's work than for the teacher to be the sole judge. Since all writers need frequent practice, a teacher cannot be expected to read everything that his or her students write. Student evaluations give teachers a chance to share the load, but, more importantly, they give students an opportunity to develop critical judgment and an appreciation for the task of writing.

The teacher (and often the students) should evaluate a lesson in terms of the objectives. Sometimes the teacher may evaluate by observing student participation. Small groups of students evaluate by choosing a composition they consider the best among several. The teacher may also collect students' papers to read aloud and discuss with the class. At other times, teachers will want to collect papers, write comments on the papers, and assign grades.

Remember that the word "evaluation" contains the word "value." Emphasize the worth of each writing attempt. By doing so, you will build students' self-esteem and ensure that students continue writing.

Some Concluding Remarks on the SAFE Lesson Plans

This book contains 33 teacher-written, classroom-tested SAFE Lesson Plans. Each SAFE Lesson Plan has a complete, fully prepared, self-contained lesson. You can select the lesson plans most appropriate for your class, and just follow the step-by-step instructions.

This book has a second purpose. We hope that teachers will adapt the "SAFE" components (**s**timulus, **a**ctivity, **f**ollow-up, and **e**valuation) to their own writing lessons for use in the classroom. We have even supplied a blank lesson plan (see page 5) to facilitate planning. First try some of the SAFE Lesson Plans in this book. Then create your own SAFE Lesson Plans, and share them with your colleagues.

Title of Lesson

Objectives   *Materials*

Students will:

1. _____

2. _____

3. _____

Stimulus   **Follow-up**

Activity   **Evaluation**

The teacher-consultants of the South Bay Writing Project have worked in many different elementary school classrooms. Our work shows us that the following ideas will help you organize your classroom writing program.

1. Give each student a file folder to decorate. Students will place all writing in these folders, stored in a file drawer or box in the classroom. In this way, you will avoid lost or discarded papers, and students will have a record of their writing achievements. At the end of each grading period, have students assess their portfolios and organize their papers for sharing with parents. Have each student staple her or his folder at the left to form a booklet to display on the desk for the classroom's "Open House."

2. Take a sample of each student's writing. Give the class a writing assignment early in the school year. Students may place their papers in their folders, but suggest that they not edit or revise this sample. Use this sample as a benchmark against which to compare their writing throughout the school year. If possible, have your class participate in a school-wide or district-wide writing assessment program.

3. Try to make sure students can perform each writing task successfully. In presenting a lesson, always begin with the prewriting warm-up. Although this is usually an oral activity, find an opportunity to write words and phrases on the chalkboard to assist students in their writing. Make a practice of providing a model for students so they will understand the assignment. You may read an example or give them copies to read. At other times students may compose one or more examples together before working independently.

4. Encourage parents to get involved in the writing program you organize. Early in the school year, advise parents of your special "campaign" to improve students' writing skills, and ask for their support. Do this by writing a letter for your students to bring home to their parents. See the letter on page 7. You may duplicate this letter on school stationery (be sure to fill in the date), or you may use it as a model for your own letter.

5. Do not expect to read everything a student writes. Students should write every day, but much of their writing should be for their own use or shared with a student audience.

6. Never grade a student's first draft. Several times each month, announce to students that you need a writing grade for your records. Each student may then choose a piece of writing from the portfolio and edit that piece to turn in. In this way, you will be grading only their best examples of writing.

7. Write with your students. It's fun to join in, and you provide a model for your students. Your participation clearly demonstrates the value you place on writing. Sharing your writing in a response group also supports the workshop atmosphere you want to cultivate. The atmosphere should suggest "we are all working together to improve our writing."

8. Create a "Publishing Center" in a corner of the room. Begin with a table, bookshelves, and lots of paper. Add pens and pencils, a typewriter, staplers, a hole punch, books, and anything else you or your students can supply to stimulate writing. Motivated students will organize a classroom or school-wide publication; encourage everyone to submit compositions for publication.

You will reach your goal of improving students' writing only if your students are self-motivated. You can help them develop such motivation. As their teacher, you can give them opportunities to write often, and you can offer them encouragement and suggestions for improvement.

Dear Parents:

I am pleased to have your child in my room this year. We will be sharing many exciting learning experiences.

We will be making a special effort to improve writing skills. I want you to understand some of the things we will be doing.

1. All children will keep a writing portfolio (folder) in which to save writing done each day. This visible record of what they have achieved will be shared with you during conferences and bound periodically as a personal anthology for each student.

2. We will take a writing sample soon to serve as a benchmark for each student. At the end of the year we will take another sample. Comparing these samples will show you and your child the growth made during the year.

3. Children will learn many different forms of writing—stories, reports, poems, plays. They will also write for different purposes—to ask for information, to express feelings, to summarize what they have learned. Some of their writing will be done in the social studies or other subject areas.

4. Children will write for different audiences—other children, themselves, you, an editor. By speaking to other people through writing, they are acquiring a "voice," a sense of themselves as having something to say. They will build their confidence and self-esteem.

5. We will talk about good writing and observe writing in books we read. Children will learn to edit their writing to improve word usage, style, and mechanics. Important selections (not everything they write) will go through several drafts as students polish their writing for publication in some way. This writing will be evaluated for grades to go on report cards.

I hope to assist the children in growing as writers and to enjoy the process.

Cordially yours,

A Talking Foundation

Students talk all the time about any number of subjects. They talk about books they have read and movies they have seen; they share problems they have at home and at school; they talk about bicycles, new clothes, and family plans. All of these discussions can lead into writing activities.

Before students begin writing, however, they need practice in focusing their ideas and clearly communicating their thoughts orally. Each lesson plan in this unit concentrates on developing a specific oral exercise that stimulates and directs a writing activity. You can extend these lessons to include writing activities, as suggested, but it's a good idea to try them first exclusively as oral exercises. The additional activities suggest other ways to highlight oral language in your classroom. When you work with the entire class, encourage all of your students to participate in the sharing of their thoughts and reactions to the stimulus you provide. Don't forget to include *your* thoughts and ideas, too.

Stamp Out Tired Words

Objectives

Students will:
1. Select words to describe a given object.
2. Use a thesaurus.
3. Find synonyms for given overused words.

Materials

crayons
blank paper
"Stamp Out Tired Words" activity sheet (p. 11)
pencils

Stimulus

1. Discuss the idea that many words are "tired" words—that they are overworked because they are used so often. Give an example: "The nice man ate the good soup." Ask students to tell you what kind of man he is, what he looks like, and what kind of soup he is eating. Explain that the words "nice" and "good" are not very meaningful, so the sentence doesn't give a clear picture of the man or of the soup.
2. Now ask your students to draw a picture of "the nice man eating the good soup," interpreting the phrase as they wish.
3. Collect the pictures. Hold up one picture at a time for the class to see, and ask if the students can think of interesting ways to describe the man and the soup, based on the picture. For example, the students might come up with sentences such as "The big, hungry man ate the delicious split pea soup" or "The friendly little old man ate the steaming hot tomato soup." Write some of the students' sentences on the chalkboard. Ask students which sentences give them the clearest picture of "the nice man eating the good soup."

Activity

1. Give each student a copy of the activity sheet. Tell the students they are going to give the words "nice" and "good" a rest.
2. Explain that *synonyms* are different words that mean almost the same thing. Brainstorm synonyms for the word "nice," and have the students list all the responses on the activity sheets. Repeat this for the word "good."

3. Show the class how to use a thesaurus to find synonyms. Ask a few students to look up the words "nice" and "good" and to read the synonyms listed, adding any that are not already listed on their activity sheets.

Follow-up

1. Have the students list other words they think are overworked and then find synonyms for these words.
2. Encourage students to use the synonyms in their daily conversation.

Evaluation

Observe student participation. Praise students who suggest words as synonyms, even if the word does not quite fit. It is important to note that, because language continually changes, many words take on different meanings. If students suggest words that don't seem to fit as synonyms, ask them to explain what the words mean to them.

Variation

Have students write sentences using some of the synonyms they list for "nice" and "good." This will help them understand how some words convey a more specific meaning than other words do.

Stamp Out Tired Words

Help get rid of these overused words!
List synonyms for each word.

_____   _____

_____   _____

_____   _____

_____   _____

_____   _____

_____   _____

_____   _____

_____   _____

_____   _____

_____   _____

nice   **good**

New Verses to an Old Song

Objective

Students will collectively write additional verses to the familiar song "She'll Be Comin' 'Round the Mountain."

Materials

"New Verses to an Old Song" song sheet (p. 13)
lined paper

Stimulus

1. Give each student a copy of the song sheet. Lead the class in singing the song.
2. Explain that the song tells a story. Ask who the song is about and what happens in each verse. Record the students' responses on the chalkboard. Some of the verses may need clarification.

Activity

1. Remind the students that this traditional song is about a journey. Explain that they will write more verses about the journey. They will first decide where the character in the song will visit next (a farm, a city, a foreign country, the moon, and so on) and will then make up appropriate verses describing various activities on the trip.
2. Call on students for ideas or for ways to word an existing idea, and help the students with the phrasing of a verse. Write the new verses on the chalkboard. (Write the first verse completely to show how the pattern matches that of the other verses. Thereafter, writing the first line of each new verse is sufficient.)
3. Have the class sing each new verse to make sure the words fit the rhythm of the song. The students may want to rearrange the verses to make a more logical story line.

4. Ask students to create appropriate hand motion to go with each new verse. Write their suggestions on the chalkboard and try out each suggestion with them. Then have the class vote on the motions they would like to include with the song.

Follow-up

Have the class learn the new verses well enough to perform their song in a program for parents and/or other students. Be sure they include their hand motions. Ask the students to teach their song to another class.

Evaluation

Observe student participation. Encourage each student to express ideas. Praise students for their creativity in writing new verses.

Variation

Have students work on their own to create new verses to another song such as "Old MacDonald Had a Farm," "Kumbaya," or "There Was an Old Lady Who Swallowed a Fly."

New Verses to an Old Song

She'll Be Comin' 'Round the Mountain

She'll be comin' 'round the mountain when she comes,
She'll be comin' 'round the mountain when she comes,
She'll be comin' 'round the mountain, she'll be comin' round
   the mountain,
She'll be comin' 'round the mountain when she comes.

She'll be drivin' six white horses when she comes,
She'll be drivin' six white horses when she comes,
She'll be drivin' six white horses, she'll be drivin' six white
   horses,
She'll be drivin' six white horses when she comes.

Oh, we'll all go out to meet her when she comes, . . .

And she'll wear her red pajamas when she comes, . . .

And we'll all have chicken and dumplings when she comes, . . .

This Is My Friend

Objectives

Students will:
1. Write a set of questions to use in an interview.
2. Interview a classmate.
3. Introduce the classmate based on information gathered in an interview.

Materials

paper bag
"This Is My Friend" activity sheet (p. 15)
pencils

Stimulus

1. Interview the principal, the librarian, or another teacher at your school. Gather information about this person that will interest your class. Consider these questions: "What is the silliest thing you have ever done?" "How do you like to spend your Saturday mornings?" "What is your favorite dessert?" and "What do you like best about your job?"
2. Invite your interviewee to class. Introduce your guest and tell about the person based on the information you gathered in your interview. After your guest leaves, explain that you learned all of this information by interviewing the person, after having prepared a set of questions. Share the questions you asked during the interview.

Activity

1. Write each student's name on a slip of paper, and put all the slips of paper into a paper bag. Have each student draw the name of a classmate to interview.
2. Help students develop interview questions. As they make a suggestion, help the students to reword the question if necessary, and write the question on the chalkboard.
3. Give each student a copy of the activity sheet. Allow about ten minutes for each student to add at least three interview questions to his or her activity sheet.
4. You will have to conduct the interviewing activity in two stages, allowing about ten minutes for each stage: at first, half the class will be interviewing while the other half is being interviewed; then the students switch roles. Everyone must interview the classmate whose name they drew.

Follow-up

1. Invite each student to come to the front of the room and introduce the classmate she or he interviewed. Remind the students that they may refer to their interview notes but that they shouldn't just read them. Set a time limit of two or three minutes to discourage rambling.
2. Have each student draw a portrait of the classmate he or she interviewed, showing some things learned about the person in the interview. Display the unlabeled portraits around the classroom and have the students try to guess who each picture represents.

Evaluation

Note whether students have elicited interesting information from their classmates during the interviews. Make sure students have asked essential questions from the interview form. Note how well students are able to identify their classmates by the student-drawn portraits.

Variation

Have students write a short composition telling what they learned about one classmate—either from the interview conducted or from another student's introduction of an interviewee.

This Is My Friend

Interview conducted by: _____

Person interviewed: _____

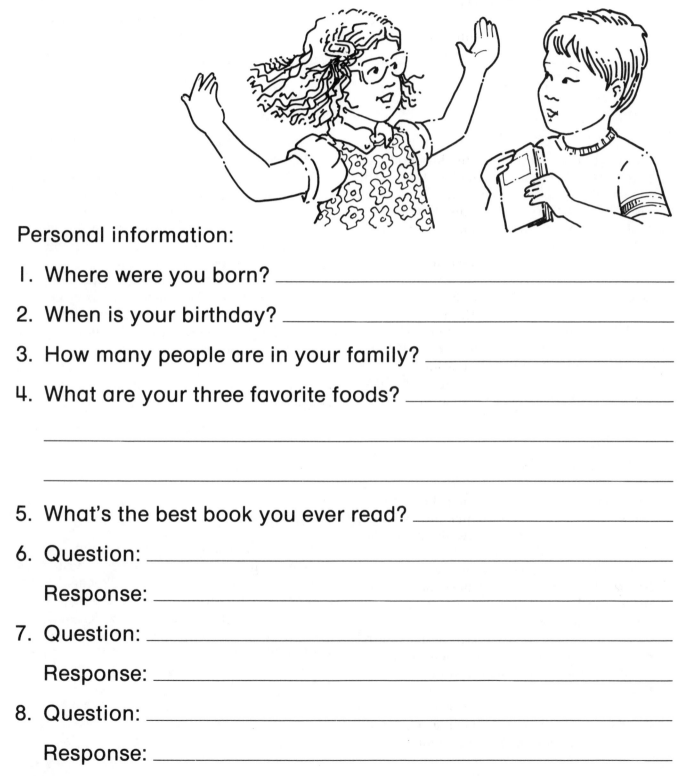

Personal information:

1. Where were you born? _____

2. When is your birthday? _____

3. How many people are in your family? _____

4. What are your three favorite foods? _____

_____

_____

5. What's the best book you ever read? _____

6. Question: _____

   Response: _____

7. Question: _____

   Response: _____

8. Question: _____

   Response: _____

Catching the Writing Express © 1987, David S. Lake Publishers

A Choral Poem: Response Poetry

Objectives

Students will:
1. Discuss the meaning of a poem.
2. Write a poem in response to the poem they read.

Materials

"A Choral Poem: Response Poetry" poem sheet (p. 17)
overhead projector
poster board
red and blue felt-tipped markers
tape recorder

Stimulus

1. Display the poem sheet on a screen using an overhead projector. Read the poem aloud, or have a few students take turns reading it once or twice.
2. Discuss what the poem means. Ask the students to think of as many different interpretations as they can.

Activity

1. Explain to the students that they are going to write a response to the poem they have just heard. Tell them that each time you read a line of the poem, you want them to volunteer a phrase that comes to mind.
2. Read the first line of the poem ("All around the world") and call on a student to respond. The response may be a rewording of the line, a clarification of what the line says, or an interpretation of the line. Write her or his response in one column on the poster board using a red marker. Example: "Everywhere I know." Ask for another response, and write this one in another column on the poster board using a blue marker. Example: "In every different country." Continue with the rest of the poem, calling on different students for their responses.
3. Point out that each set of lines they contributed makes a poem. Read the "red" poem; then read the "blue" poem.
4. Divide the class into three groups. Have one group recite the "red" poem, one group recite the "blue" poem, and another group recite the original poem on the poem sheet.

Follow-up

1. Tape-record the students reading each poem. Play back the tape so the students can listen.
2. Note whether the students' new lines relate the same meaning as the original poem. They need not, but the poems as a whole should convey a similar meaning. Comparing the meanings of the three poems will provide an interesting topic of discussion.
3. Repeat this lesson using other poems your students like. After they have learned the procedure, your students may work independently, on their own or in small groups, to write response poems.

Evaluation

Praise students' efforts. At times, guide the students to rephrase their responses for more meaningful expressions.

Variation

Together as a group, write one response poem. As one student gives a response line, write it on the poster board or on the chalkboard. Allow two or three minutes for each student to think of another response line and write it down. After you have completed the activity, each student will have his or her own response poem to read aloud to the class.

All around the world
There are children like me,
In many strange places
They happen to be.

They eat and they sleep,
They run and they play,
They work and are helpful
Day by day.

Their dress and their food
Are different from mine;
Their homes and their customs
Are hard to define.

But all 'round the world
They're still just like me
In living and giving.
Good friends are we.

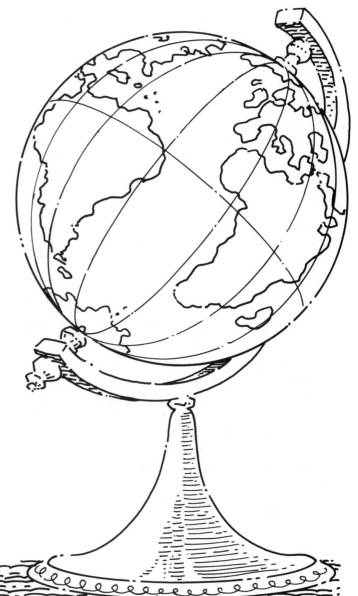

Poetry Corner

Establish a poetry corner in the classroom. Use the poetry corner to display favorite poems and seasonal poems. Present a new poem each week for the students to learn. Display the poem on a poster board chart. Introduce the poem on Monday, reading it to the class a couple of times and then asking the students to join in, reading it aloud with you. If you repeat the poetry reading each day of the week, by Friday most of the students will know the poem by heart. Begin with repetitive poems, short poems, or poems that have a clear rhyming pattern. These are the easiest to learn and will help students internalize sentence patterns.

Sharing Time

Assign a topic for sharing, such as "something red" or "measuring tools," and have students bring an object to class to represent the topic. Ask each student to tell two or more important facts about his or her object. Use sharing time topics that relate to the curriculum.

Playground Songs

Elementary school students often recite chants and sing songs to accompany games. Have the students demonstrate the songs and chants they know. Give them an opportunity to show any hand motions that go with the songs, or to play the games that the songs accompany. With the students, write the words to the songs or chants, comparing variations.

As a homework assignment, have the students ask grown-ups at home if they remember songs, rhymes, or chants from their childhood (such as jump-rope jingles or rhymes to accompany jacks). Compile a notebook with the songs the students bring to class. Encourage students to borrow collections of singing games, jump-rope rhymes, and hand games from the library.

Riddle Day

Invite students to bring riddles to share. (They may learn the riddles from a book, but they should be able to tell the riddle rather than read it.) You may wish to set a limit on how many riddles each student may tell. Keep a tally of how many riddles puzzled the class. Have the students write their riddles, omitting the answers. Make a class riddle book.

Class Newsletter

Help your students issue a periodic newsletter that includes student-written articles about school or classroom events, student-written cartoons and essays, student art, and student-conducted interviews. Every few weeks, appoint a new group of students to be responsible for compiling an issue of the newsletter. Help the groups collect articles and set up the newsletter. Make enough copies of each newsletter so that students can share it with their families. Keep copies of each newsletter in a loose-leaf binder in the classroom, and encourage students to reread past issues later in the school year.

Getting Started Writing

Initial writing activities should be structured very carefully so that students know exactly what is expected of them. Modeling the activity with students is important, and showing students a sample of the finished product is desirable. This does not mean that all the writing will be identical; there **is** room for individuality and creativity in each lesson.

In the beginning stages of the writing program students may need to be guided through each step of the writing process. Consider conducting lessons on descriptive writing in the beginning stages of your writing program. Most children find it easier to describe physical objects and then build up to describing more abstract things as they develop their skills and their confidence. It will be rewarding for you to watch their progress as they develop into competent, creative, and expressive writers.

Objects

Objectives

Students will:
1. List words associated with a given object.
2. Choose an object and list words associated with that object.

Materials

"Objects" activity sheet (p. 21)
lined paper
crayons or felt-tipped markers
construction paper
glue

Stimulus

1. Draw an outline of an apple on the chalkboard. Make it large enough to write at least twenty words inside the shape.
2. Elicit words that the students think are associated with apples. Discuss each word. Ask students to tell how the word relates to apples. Encourage students to stretch their imaginations and name words and even phrases that are only remotely related to apples. Examples: "red, green, smooth, round, stem, core, seeds, juicy, autumn, crunchy, sauce, cider, Johnny Appleseed, banana, pear, peach, dried, dumplings, worm, hole, fragrant, growing, school, lunch, sweet, tart, sour, star, cook, stomachache, caramel." It's important to keep writing as long as your students continue naming words and phrases.

Activity

1. Give each student a copy of the activity sheet, which shows an outline of a house, or have each student draw the outline of another object on a sheet of lined paper.
2. Have students work individually to list words associated with the house (or other object they have drawn). Tell the students to do their best with spelling, using what they know about letters and sounds, and using a dictionary. Urge them to keep writing even if they don't know the exact spelling of a word; you can help them to correct their spelling later.

Follow-up

Have students cut out the objects and mount them on colored construction paper. Display the papers on a bulletin board so the whole class can enjoy reading the words their classmates associate with common objects.

Evaluation

Check students' understanding of the words they list. Ask students to explain the association of some words to the object pictured.

Variations

1. Have students draw three outlines of the same object and list nouns inside one outline, verbs inside another, and adjectives inside a third outline.
2. Divide the class into groups of three or four students. Give the groups a selection of "object" possibilities related to science or social studies topics they are currently studying. Have the students in each group choose an object, make a large outline of the object, and list as many words associated with that object as they can. The groups should work on this project over several days, using reference materials to find more words.

SAFE Lesson Plan *Shoes*

Objectives

Students will:
1. List words to describe various types of shoes.
2. Write a story about shoes.

Materials

"The Elves and the Shoesmaker" story (p. 23)
"Shoes" activity sheet (p. 24)
pencils

Stimulus

1. Read "The Elves and the Shoemaker" aloud to the class.
2. Gather the students in a circle on the floor. Sit with them and share experiences they have had with shoes. Ask what kind of shoes they wear in summer and what kind they wear in winter. Do they have special party shoes? Do they get to shop for their own shoes? Have they ever worn shoes that were too small or too large?
3. Have each student take off one shoe and leave it in the middle of the circle. Select several different types of shoes for everyone to examine and discuss. Discuss the parts of a shoe. Leave the students' shoes in the circle.
4. Brainstorm words to define various types of shoes (such as sandals, boots, jelly shoes, oxfords, sneakers, high-tops, deck shoes, moccasins, and so on), or to describe specific shoes (such as dirty, shiny, polished, leather, canvas, and so on). As the students call out words, write them on the chalkboard.

Activity

Have students return to their desks. Give each student a copy of the activity sheet, and direct the students to write a story about shoes. Encourage them to think about their favorite kind of shoes, where they like to wear those shoes, how the shoes look and feel, where and when they purchased the shoes. Students should use at least two of the words listed on the chalkboard as well as their own ideas. They may

continue their stories on the back of the activity sheet if they need more writing space. As students complete their stories, they may collect their shoes.

Follow-up

Have students pair up and read their stories to their partners. Encourage students to read their stories aloud to the entire class.

Evaluation

Collect the stories and read them. Note how well each student was able to use the ideas discussed and the words listed on the chalkboard. Praise the use of original ideas and the creative use of words.

Variations

1. Have students make a classroom collection of as many different kinds of shoes as they can. Pass out the shoes and have each student write about the shoe he or she gets. Students may write descriptions, stories, or even dialogue between that shoe and one of their own.
2. Substitute the book *Brand New Shoes*, by Eve Rice, for the story "The Elves and the Shoemaker."

1. pick 1 pair
2. where they went   adventure
3. how they looked & felt

The Elves and the Shoemaker

Once there was a shoemaker who made shoes—and made them well. Yet, luck was against him. Although he worked very hard, he became poorer and poorer until he had nothing left but enough leather for one pair of shoes.

That evening he cut out the leather for the last pair of shoes. Then after laying the pieces in a neat row on his workbench, he went peacefully to bed. "I'll get up early in the morning," he thought. "Then I can finish the shoes and perhaps sell them."

But when he woke up, the pieces of cut leather were nowhere to be seen. In their place stood a pair of beautiful shoes, finished to the last seam. The shoemaker was amazed. He did not know what to make of it, but he picked up the shoes and set them out for sale. Soon a man came and bought the shoes. Because he was so pleased with their fine quality, he paid more than the usual price for them. With this money, the shoemaker was able to buy enough leather for two pairs of shoes.

As before, he cut out the leather for the next day's sewing, laid it on his workbench, and went to bed. In the morning, there were the shoes—two pairs this time! The shoemaker didn't know how such a thing could happen, but he was pleased. Again, he was lucky enough to sell the shoes for more than the usual price. This time he was able to buy enough leather for four pairs of shoes.

Well, so it went on. Night after night he cut out leather and laid it on his workbench. And morning after morning there stood a row of handsome shoes. At last the shoemaker was no longer poor. In fact, he became a wealthy man, with enough money in his pockets to buy whatever he needed.

Then one evening the shoemaker decided to find out who or what was making the shoes during the night. The shoemaker's wife lit a candle and set it on a table. Then she hid behind the curtains with her husband. Just before midnight, two stout little elves, wearing ragged and tattered clothes, sprang up on the workbench and began making shoes. They worked so swiftly and skillfully that the man and his wife could hardly believe their eyes. The next morning, the wife said to her husband, "Those elves have made us rich, but they themselves are so poor. I will make them some clothes and knit them each a pair of stockings. You can make them each a pair of little shoes."

And so one evening, when everything was ready, they placed their presents on the workbench instead of the leather. Then they hid behind the curtains and waited.

At midnight, there came the two elves, skipping along, ready to work as usual. But they saw no leather. They looked again and spied the little garments lying on the workbench. At first they seemed puzzled. When they finally realized that the clothes were meant for them, they were filled with joy. They laughed with delight and sang, "Now we are smart gentlemen. Why should we ever work again?" When they were fully dressed, they skipped away.

They never came back, but the shoemaker and his wife were always lucky after that. And they never forgot the two little elves who had helped them in their time of need.

Shoes

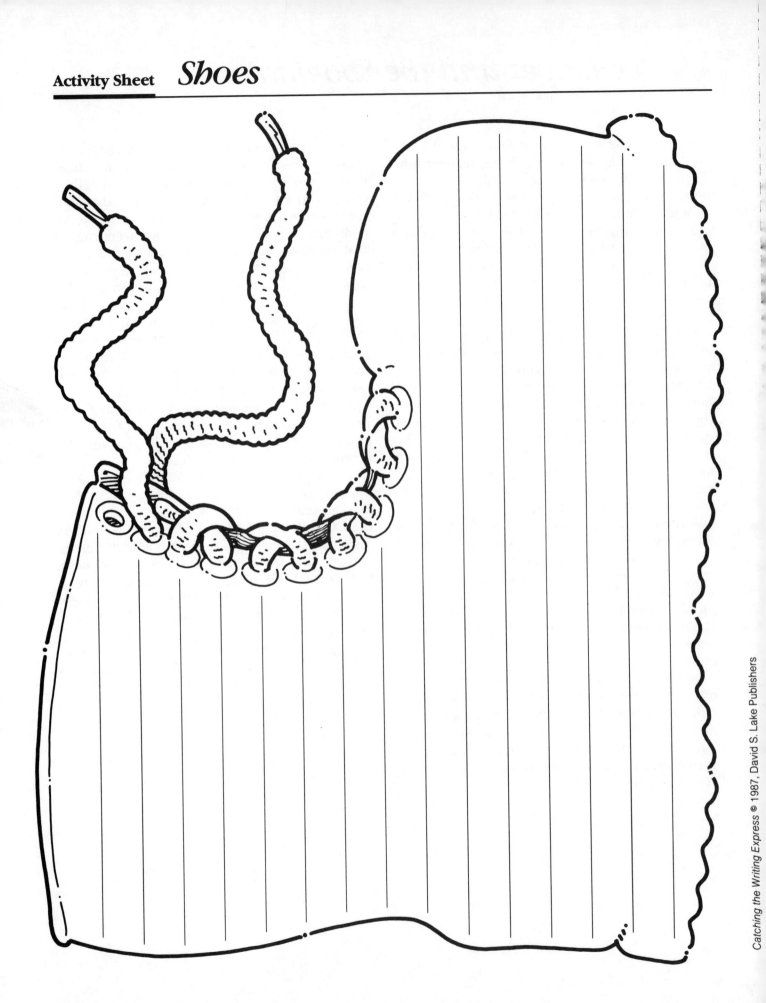

From the Point of View of a Chair

Objectives

Students will:
1. Describe a chair without naming it.
2. Try to recognize a chair from its description.
3. Write a paragraph about a chair from the chair's point of view.

Materials

three different types of chairs
"From the Point of View of a Chair" activity sheet (p. 26)

Stimulus

Place three different types of chairs (a beanbag chair, a folding lawn chair, a rocking chair, a straight-backed chair) in the front of the classroom. Discuss the similarities and differences between the chairs. Invite students to come to the front of the classroom and sit in each chair, noting how each one feels. Discuss the uses of each kind of chair. Ask the students how they think each kind of chair might feel about the use it receives.

Activity

1. Give each student a copy of the activity sheet. Have each student select one chair to write about. They may choose to write about one of the chairs pictured on the activity sheet or one of the actual chairs used in the stimulus exercise.
2. Direct students to write a paragraph about the chair from the chair's point of view, without identifying the chair they are writing about. Students may describe the chair, as if the chair were describing itself, and may tell what it feels like when someone sits on it. Students may also talk about other ways in which the chair is used—as a clothes rack, a place to store objects, a stepping stool, a scratching post for a cat, or a footrest—and how it feels to be used in this way.

Follow-up

1. Divide the class into small groups. Each student will read her or his paragraph aloud to the group, and the other members of the group will try to guess which chair the paragraph is about. Have each group select the paragraph that was hardest to guess.
2. Have each student question the members of the group to find out which words in their paragraphs give clues to the identity of the chair described.

Evaluation

Have each student perform a self-evaluation, keeping track of how many classmates were able to identify which chair was the subject of the paragraph and underlining the "giveaway" words in the paragraph.

Variation

Use other objects such as boxes (cereal box, gift box, jewelry box, music box, toy box) or spoons (silver teaspoon, wooden spoon, plastic spoon, slotted spoon, serving spoon) instead of chairs.

From the Point of View of a Chair

_____

_____

_____

_____

_____

_____

_____

_____

_____

_____

_____

_____

Catching the Writing Express © 1987, David S. Lake Publishers

Scenic Poems

Objectives

Students will:
1. Select words to describe a scenic picture.
2. Arrange descriptive words to create a free-verse poem.

Materials

old magazines that feature pictures, such as *National Geographic, Smithsonian,* or *Better Homes and Gardens*
construction paper
scissors
glue

Stimulus

1. Choose a scenic picture from a magazine. Display the picture so that everyone in the class can see it. Point out color contrasts, textures, and the mood of the picture.
2. Ask students to describe the picture, using precise words as well as general words. Ask them to describe everything they see and also to tell what the picture reminds them of. List the descriptive words they name (at least 25 descriptive words).
3. Have the students help you choose words and arrange them in a pleasing pattern to create a poem. Read the phrases aloud so the students can hear the poetic sounds of the description.
4. Choose another picture and repeat the procedure. Make sure students understand how the descriptive vocabulary fits each picture.

Activity

1. Have each student select a magazine and choose a scenic picture from the magazine. Direct students to cut out the picture and glue it to a piece of construction paper, leaving space to add a poem.
2. Have students look through their magazines again, this time looking for individual words that describe their scenes. Students should find at least fifteen words, cut them out, and arrange them to create a free-verse poem. Have students glue the words onto the construction paper when they have found an arrangement that pleases them.

Follow-up

1. Invite each student to stand in front of the class, hold up the scenic picture, and then read her or his poem aloud to the class.
2. Gather the scenic poems and pictures into a booklet. Students may read the poems in their free time. They may wish to share the booklet of scenic poems with another class.

Evaluation

As students read their poems aloud, note whether the descriptive words they use are appropriate to the picture chosen. Comment on the arrangement of words to create a meaningful free-verse poem.

Variations

1. Have students list descriptive words instead of trying to find them in magazines. If students write the words on small pieces of paper, they will still be able to manipulate the pieces of paper to try various arrangements of words.
2. Suggest that each student write a paragraph rather than a poem to describe the picture. Students should still list descriptive words and use these words in their paragraphs.

Popcorn Clusters

Objectives

Students will:
1. Brainstorm words associated with a given topic.
2. Write a paragraph on a chosen topic.

Materials

hot-air popcorn popper (optional)
popcorn (optional)
bowls (optional)
five-minute timer
"Popcorn Clusters" activity sheet
  (p. 29)
lined paper
pencils

Stimulus

1. If possible, make popcorn for the class. Point out how the kernels of corn pop—slowly at first and then rapidly and in all directions. If it is not practical to make popcorn in the classroom, ask students to describe how popcorn pops.
2. Explain that in this exercise students are going to "play popcorn" with words. The purpose of this exercise is to name many words for a given topic as quickly as possible.
3. Write the word "popcorn" on the chalkboard. Set the timer for four minutes. Direct students to name words that come to mind. Record the words on the chalkboard. (Ask a student to help you record the words, because the responses may come too fast.) Stop when the timer signals, even if the students have not finished naming words. Tally the number of words, and write the number on the chalkboard.

Activity

1. Give each student a copy of the activity sheet. Tell them that they will try this "popcorn" exercise on their own now. Explain that they should be concerned only with recording as many words and short phrases as possible within the time limit, and that they need not be concerned with spelling or form. Also explain that when the timer signals, the students must put their pencils down immediately.
2. Write a stimulus word (lunch, pet, mountain, tree, bug, water) on the chalkboard. Set the timer for two minutes, and tell the students to begin.
3. Have students tally their words and phrases and write the number at the top of the activity sheet.

Follow-up

1. Ask students to volunteer to share the words and phrases they wrote down. List some of the students' responses on the chalkboard. Discuss the variety of words and the range of ideas reflected.
2. Have each student write a paragraph about the topic (the stimulus word), using at least five words listed on his or her activity sheet.

Evaluation

Note how well the words and phrases on a student's activity sheet relate to the topic word. Consider giving a prize to the student who lists the highest number of words and phrases.

Repeat this activity throughout the school year. You will probably see the list of words increase for all students. The fluency in the students' paragraphs is also likely to increase.

Write your main topic in the biggest piece of popcorn.
Add popcorn clusters as needed.

Composing Class Rules

After conducting a class discussion on the need for rules at school, direct each student to write five rules for classroom behavior. Select several students to read their rules aloud. Ask two other students to take turns recording the rules on the chalkboard, placing a check mark beside a rule each time it is mentioned again.

Tally the rules most frequently cited. Ask your students if these are the most important rules for their class. Ask them to suggest any other rules they feel should be included on the list. Have the class vote on the five rules most important to the class.

Talk about the importance of wording rules in a positive manner. ("Walk in the classroom" is more positive than "No running in the classroom.") Have the students brainstorm ways to word all the class rules in a positive tone.

Special Day Menus

List a few "special occasion" days, such as Mother's Day, Halloween, and Valentine's Day, on the chalkboard. Ask the students to suggest other special days—established ones or made-up ones. List these on the chalkboard also.

Discuss menus. Explain that a menu at home includes all of the foods that will be served during that meal. (A menu at a restaurant, on the other hand, lists all of the foods available.) Show samples of dinner party menus from cookbooks or cooking magazines.

Have the students select a special day from the list on the chalkboard and plan a menu for a meal related to that special day. Example: for St. Patrick's Day, the menu might include shamrock salad, leprechaun lamb stew, Irish soda bread, Blarney Stone pudding, and Belfast root beer. Have the students copy their menus on fine paper, glue them to construction paper, and decorate them. Display the menus on a bulletin board. Give the students an opportunity to read their menus to the class and discuss the appropriateness of each food to the special day.

What If?

Write a "what if?" question on the chalkboard. Some examples are: "What if you came to school and saw no one on the playground?" "What if the stores ran out of food?" or "What if summer vacation lasted a whole year?" Have students respond twice to the question, first in a serious way and then in a nonsensical or whimsical way. This will challenge them to be creative as well as sensible.

As a separate activity, have each student write three "what if?" questions. At least one question should be serious, and at least one should be fantastic. Collect these, share them with the class, and keep them to use for writing assignments during the school year.

Students Feeling Good About Themselves

Boosting students' self-esteem is one of the most important and challenging objectives for teachers to achieve. Writing helps identify and develop special inner abilities that build self-esteem. When students begin to express their thoughts in writing, they must first think about who they are.

The lessons in this unit help students to explore their own thoughts and feelings. They also give students an opportunity to get to know one another better. Students will be asked to keep a journal to record their feelings about their likes and dislikes, about family and friends, and about whatever occupies their thoughts. Keeping a journal is a good way for students to notice the changes they are experiencing.

Games with Names

Objectives

Students will:
1. Think of words that rhyme with their own names.
2. Write a short poem.

Materials

lined paper
blank paper
crayons
pencils

Stimulus

Begin by having students suggest words that rhyme with your first or last name. It is harder to find rhyming words for some names, so you must be a little flexible about how close the rhymes are. Here are some examples:

JANE: plane, main, train, strain, chain, plain, crane, rain
LISA: pizza, "freeza," "teasa," "please ya"
WALKER: talker, clocker, stocker, rocker, knocker, soccer

After coming up with rhyming words, work with the students to write a poem about you. The poem will probably be funny, but try to make it at least a little accurate. Write the poem on the chalkboard so that lines can be changed or rearranged easily. You should have at least six lines in the finished piece. Copy the poem onto a sheet of paper and illustrate it or have students illustrate it.

Activity

1. Give each student a sheet of lined paper. Divide the class into groups of three or four students. Have each group work together to come up with words that rhyme with the first or last name of each member of the group. Once students have a list of rhyming words for their names, they're on their own for the actual writing.

2. Have students return to their desks and work independently to write their name poems. Suggest that the students think of funny descriptions about themselves as one approach to writing the poem. It's usually easier to come up with comical rhymes than serious ones.

Follow-up

Have students copy their poems on clean lined paper and draw self-portraits to complement the poems. Display the poems and self-portraits on a bulletin board.

Evaluation

Observe student participation in finding rhyming words. When you read the poem, look for rhyming patterns, poetry format, and length of poems (each poem should have at least six lines).

Variation

Use friends, family members, familiar book characters, or historical figures as subjects of the poems.

Familiar Faces

Objectives

Students will:
1. Think about action-oriented goals they would like to accomplish.
2. List words to describe action.
3. Write a descriptive paragraph about an action-oriented goal.

Materials

a photograph of each student
scissors
blank paper
crayons
glue
lined paper
poster board
felt-tipped marker
pencils

Stimulus

1. Lead a discussion about goals and dreams for the future. Ask students to imagine what they would do if they could do anything in the world. Have them tell about activities they are involved in now, such as Little League, violin lessons, or raising rabbits. Ask what they would like to accomplish in the next ten years, whether related to the activities they now participate in or a different interest. Students may suggest realistic accomplishments (such as learning to fly an airplane) or fantastic accomplishments (such as growing wings to fly with).
2. List on the chalkboard the action verbs mentioned as the students talk about these accomplishments—plausible or wholly imaginary.
3. Make a photocopy of the students' photographs. Cut them apart and give each student the photocopy of his or her photograph and a sheet of blank paper. Ask the students to make portraits of themselves engaged in the activity they would like to accomplish. Rather than drawing their faces in the portraits, they should glue the copies of their photographs on the sheets of paper. The pictures should stress action.

Activity

1. Give each student two sheets of lined paper, and have the student list words to describe the action in her or his self-portrait.
2. Direct students to write a paragraph about the self-portrait. They should write about the activity portrayed, the setting, what they look like in the portrait, and how they feel in the situation pictured.

Follow-up

1. Have students read their paragraphs to a partner. The partner should listen for and list the action words in the paragraph.
2. Make a master list on poster board of action words used by the students in their paragraphs.

Evaluation

Praise students for their effective use of action verbs and descriptive passages. Note how well the students' paragraphs reflect their self-portraits.

Wishes

Objectives

Students will:
1. List, by category, things they would like to wish for.
2. Write a composition about three wishes.

Materials

"Wishes" activity sheet (p. 35)
lined paper
pencils

Stimulus

1. Begin with class discussion. Ask students to think about what they would wish for if they were granted three wishes. Write all their suggestions on the chalkboard.
2. Take a few minutes to have students classify the ideas on the board according to the kinds of wishes. Group together all wishes for possessions, all wishes for a better world, all wishes for happiness, and all fantasy wishes (such as being able to fly or to see through walls). The first list will probably be the longest.
3. Ask students to think about what is very important to them in life. What would they really miss if they didn't have it? What kinds of things are they looking forward to being able to do? Discuss friendship, family, and health. Have students volunteer their responses to these questions, but don't write them down.

Activity

1. Give each student a copy of the activity sheet. Direct students to write several ideas for each wish category. Remind them that no idea is too farfetched for a wish.
2. When students have completed the activity sheet, they should underline their three favorite wishes. Stipulate that only one wish can be from the "material gains" category.

3. Give each student a sheet of lined paper. Have each student write a paragraph (or at least two sentences) about each wish, describing the wish and telling why he or she chose it.

Follow-up

1. Have students read their compositions to the whole class. Display the paragraphs along with the activity sheets on a bulletin board entitled "I Wish, I Wish."
2. Ask students to vote on the wishes they feel are most creative, most beneficial to society, and so on.

Evaluation

Read each composition. Make sure that students included only one "material gains" wish. Also look at each activity sheet to perceive how well students understood the categorizing process.

Wishes

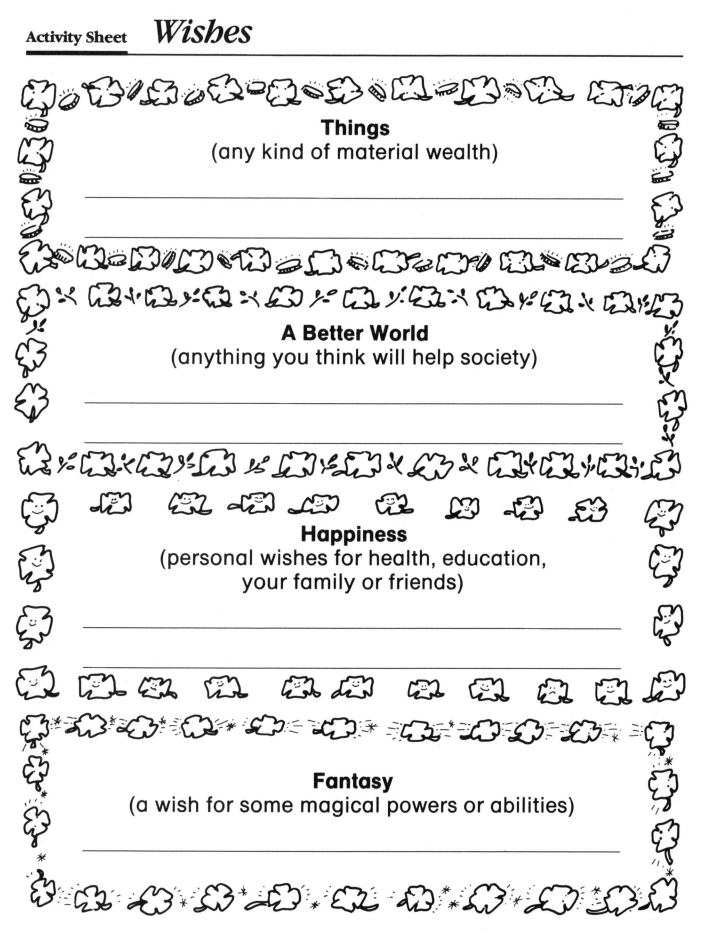

Things
(any kind of material wealth)

_____

_____

A Better World
(anything you think will help society)

_____

_____

Happiness
(personal wishes for health, education,
your family or friends)

_____

_____

Fantasy
(a wish for some magical powers or abilities)

_____

Memory Writing

Objectives

Students will:
1. Briefly describe personal experiences they remember.
2. Write a story about one personal experience.

Materials

I Used To, by Sonia Lisker
"Memory Writing" activity sheet (p. 37)
lined paper
pencils

Stimulus

1. Read *I Used To* aloud to the class.
2. Prepare a statement you can use as a model introduction for telling a personal experience. (Example: "Hi, I'm Mr. Johnson, and when I was a little boy my favorite game was marbles.") Give your model statement.
3. Then have the students introduce themselves and give a brief account of a past experience.

Activity

1. Give each student a copy of the activity sheet. Have the students complete each sentence on the page, telling about a different experience each time. This portion of the activity makes a good homework assignment.
2. Divide the class into small groups and have the students in each group read aloud the sentences on their activity sheets. The students will help each group member to select one experience to write about by voting on the experience they think makes the best story.
3. Have the students return to their desks to complete the paragraph writing on their own. Give each student two sheets of lined paper. The students should first jot down everything

they can remember about the experience briefly described on the activity sheet. Then each student will write a story based on the experience. Remind students that they can add to their "brainstorm" lists even if they are already in the middle of writing the story. Also remind them that they don't have to include everything listed on their "brainstorm" lists.

Follow-up

Have students return to their small groups and share their stories with one another. Then have the students discuss the experiences and find out if other students in the class have had similar experiences.

Evaluation

Have students in each group choose their favorite story and read it aloud to the class. Discuss how each author used descriptive words. Also collect the activity sheets and note whether students filled in all of the sections.

Memory Writing

When I was a baby I used to:

_____

_____

After I learned to walk I used to:

_____

_____

After I learned to talk I used to:

_____

_____

When I was in kindergarten I used to:

_____

_____

Last year I used to:

_____

_____

My Favorite Place in the World

Objectives

Students will:
1. Identify the three parts of a letter.
2. Imagine a place they would like to visit.
3. Write a letter to their parents.

Materials

travel brochures showing pictures of tourist spots
blank paper
crayons or felt-tipped pens
"My Favorite Place in the World" activity sheet (p. 39)
lined paper
envelopes
pencils

Stimulus

1. Bring travel brochures and pictures of places to visit, and share them with the class. They could be of local attractions, places mentioned in your reading or social studies texts, places you have visited, or places featured in the travel section of a newspaper or magazine.
2. Ask the students to consider where they would go if they could go anywhere in the world. Elicit ideas about places they might like to visit. Students may suggest visiting familiar places such as a grandparent or other relative's home or a past vacation site. Encourage students to consider totally new and unfamiliar places.
3. Give each student a sheet of blank paper and ask the students to draw a picture of the place they'd like to visit. Point out that they will have to make up the details in the picture if they have not visited that place.
4. Review letter format, and provide a model on a chart.

Activity

1. Give each student a copy of the activity sheet. Explain that in this activity they will write letters to their parents, describing the places they want to visit, giving the reasons why, and asking permission to take such a trip. Students should use the activity sheet as a rough draft, clustering ideas and details.

2. Have each student share the rough draft with a classmate for editing and content suggestions before turning it in to you.
3. When both of you are satisified with content and form, each student may copy his or her letter in final form on clean lined paper. Stress the importance of neatness when writing letters.

Follow-up

1. Have students share their letters with the rest of the class. Students may list where each person wants to visit.
2. Have each student address an envelope and enclose the letter and picture in the envelope. Have students take the letters home to their parents. You might want to encourage parents to answer the letters they receive. Each student could then write another letter, imagining they have already visited the favorite place, and thanking their parents for that opportunity. This would give students practice in writing thank-you notes.

Evaluation

Read each letter to be sure it includes the place and the reason for wanting to visit as well as making sure it's in correct letter form.

My Favorite Place in the World

I. Letter Form

Date _____

Dear _____
(Opening)

_____
(Body of letter)

_____

_____

_____

_____
(Closing)

_____
(Signature)

2. Envelope Form

From:

_____
Name (first and last)

_____
Street address

_____
City, State, ZIP code

To:

_____
Name

_____
Street address

_____
City, State, ZIP code

Stamp

Kind Words

Distribute a small square of paper to each student and ask the students to write their names on the paper and to fold the paper in fourths. Collect the papers, put them in a box or a hat, shake them up, and have each student draw a name. (You may include your own name in the drawing.) Distribute writing paper and direct each student to write all the good things about the person whose name she or he drew, identifying that person by name. The students should not write their own names on the papers. Collect the papers and read them aloud before giving each one to the person written about. It's such a treat to hear nice things about yourself and not even know who wrote them!

Student of the Week

Plan a "Student of the Week" bulletin board in your classroom. Prepare a space that you can use all year. Draw your students' names from a hat for the sequence, and then tell the students what you have planned.

Each week, put a large sheet of blank paper on the bulletin board and write the name of the student honored as Student of the Week. Have that student decorate the "Student of the Week" bulletin board space as desired. Suggest that the students bring baby pictures of themselves, photos of their families and friends, or items that can be attached to the bulletin board that express their personalities. Students may list their hobbies or their favorite colors, foods, songs, and books on the blank sheet of paper. During the week, the other students in the class may write special messages on the bulletin board paper about the Student of the Week. At the end of the week, have the honored student read aloud all the things written by the other students.

Writing about Personal Feelings

Tell your class a personal story about a time when you were really scared. It could be a recent incident or an incident from when you were your students' age. Begin the story, "I was really scared when . . ."

Ask your students to try to remember a time when they were really scared. Don't let them relate their stories aloud yet! Ask the students to write their stories first. Then they may tell about their frightening experiences (or they may read their stories aloud). Collect the stories and bind them into a book entitled "Boy, Was I Scared!"

This activity may be adapted for different types of experiences and for different emotions. It may be repeated throughout the school year. This type of writing activity helps students see that they are not alone in their emotions.

Having Fun with Books

In addition to being great fun and a wonderful model of language, reading books aloud provides numerous ideas to stimulate writing. Students can imitate or extend patterns, rewrite familiar stories from another point of view, change story endings, and imitate an author's writing style. Reading stimulates thought and generates enthusiasm about writing.

As you read through this section, think of books you enjoy reading to your students, and see how you can fit them into your writing program. After you've tried some of the following lessons you'll undoubtedly think of new ways to use your favorite books in the classroom. Reading is a natural starting point for writers.

It Looked Like . . .

Objectives

Students will:
1. Identify a pattern presented in a book.
2. Write similes following a pattern sentence to describe a cloud.

Materials

"Clouds" reference sheet (p. 43)
It Looked Like Spilt Milk, by Charles G. Shaw
"It Looked Like . . ." activity sheet (p. 44)
blue construction paper
scissors
glue
shredded newspaper
stapler
string
pencils

Stimulus

This is a good activity to try when studying weather.
1. Give each student a copy of the "Clouds" reference sheet. (You may wish to have students identify the basic cloud type in each illustration.) Spend some time outdoors with the class viewing cloud patterns. Ask the students to notice the shapes of various clouds.
2. Read *It Looked Like Spilt Milk* aloud to the class. Emphasize the sentence pattern in the book. Ask the students what shapes they have seen in clouds. List their responses on the chalkboard.

Activity

Give each student a copy of the activity sheet. Each will complete the sentence on the page, writing a creative statement (a simile) about what a certain cloud looks like to them, imitating the pattern in Charles Shaw's book. Students should use scratch paper or the back of the "Clouds" reference sheet as they brainstorm ideas, reserving their activity sheet for the final copy of the sentence.

Follow-up

1. Give students sheets of construction paper. Each student should hold the construction paper and the activity sheet together and cut out the cloud shape, cutting through both sheets of paper. The student will then glue the activity sheet cloud shape to the construction paper cloud shape, gluing only around the edges but leaving an opening. When the glue has dried, help students to stuff their paper clouds with shredded newspaper and staple the opening shut.

2. Attach a piece of string to each cloud and hang the clouds from the ceiling.

Evaluation

Have students read one another's sentences on the stuffed clouds and decide on their favorite expressions. Check each cloud to see that it follows the sentence pattern modeled. Praise imaginative cloud-shape descriptions.

It Looked Like . . .

Complete the sentence below to describe a cloud you have seen. Be creative, and be specific. Here is an example:

It looked like a giant's footprint pressed deeply into the blue of the sky, but it wasn't a giant's footprint.

It looked like _____

_____

_____ ,

but it wasn't _____ .

School Days and Weekends

Objectives

Students will:

1. Compare and contrast school-day activities with weekend activities
2. Write one paragraph about school days and one about weekends, describing an activity that typifies each type of day.

Materials

Summer Is . . . by Charlotte Zolotow
"School Days and Weekends" activity sheet (p. 46)
pencils

Stimulus

1. Read *Summer Is . . .* aloud to the class. Ask your students to suggest what summer means to them. The statements they make will be *metaphors* for summer. Point out statements that were mentioned in the book and those that are new. Explain that everyone has different experiences, which is why the word "summer" may mean something different to everyone.

2. Write the headings "School Days" and "Weekends" on the chalkboard. Ask the students to name activities for each category. Point out similarities and differences between the two lists.

Activity

1. Give each student a copy of the activity sheet. Have students make a chart on the back of this sheet, listing several school-day activities and several weekend activities in which they participate.

2. Each student may choose one activity from each category and write about the activities to create metaphors for school days and weekends. (Example: "School days are talking with my friends at recess.") The student will then elaborate on the topic, describing the activity in greater detail and telling what he or she likes about that activity.

Follow-up

Have the students illustrate each activity and then share their paragraphs. Collect the pages and collate them into a class book. Encourage students to read the book during free time.

Evaluation

Check whether students followed the pattern presented on the activity sheet. As a class, examine the students' lists of school-day activities and weekend activities. Ask which activities could belong to both categories and which belong only to the given category. Be prepared for disagreement on some, and encourage students to back up their opinions.

Variation

Adapt this activity to compare different meals, different school subjects, different sports, and so on.

School Days and Weekends

Describe each type of day. Write about an activity that you think stands for that type of day.

School days are _____

_____

_____

_____

_____

Weekends are _____

_____

_____

_____

_____

Draw a picture to show the activity for each type of day.

Catching the Writing Express © 1987, David S. Lake Publishers

Tear-Water Tea

Objectives

Students will:
1. List "silly-sad" experiences with a group.
2. Write and illustrate a list of things that would help them make tears for "tear-water tea."

Materials

"Tear-Water Tea" from *Owl at Home,* by Arnold Lobel
"Tear-Water Tea" activity sheet (p. 48)
herbal tea or friendship tea (see the recipe)
plastic cups
pencils

Stimulus

1. Read "Tear-Water Tea" aloud to your class. Ask the students to name some of the things that made Owl cry. List these things on the chalkboard. Discuss the kinds of things Owl thought about to make tears for his tea. Point out that he cried over "silly-sad" things such as a pencil that was too short to write with or mashed potatoes left on a plate because no one wanted to eat them.

2. Ask students what "silly-sad" things they would think about in order to fill a teacup with tears. Record their ideas on the chalkboard, encouraging students to give complete ideas, such as a tube of toothpaste with a hole in it so the toothpaste comes out of the wrong end, an ice-cream cone that is empty because the ice cream scoops have fallen out, a pencil without an eraser so people can't fix their mistakes.

Activity

Give each student a copy of the activity sheet. Tell students that they should write a list of things they would think about to fill a teacup full of tears. Suggest these examples: "I could fill a teacup with tears if I didn't have a costume for Halloween; if no one ate the tomatoes from my garden." Students should list at least four ideas. They can then illustrate each idea in one of the teacups around the pot.

Follow-up

1. This would be a wonderful time to have a class tea party! Have students read their lists aloud while sipping herbal or "friendship" tea.

"Friendship Tea"

2 cups powdered orange-flavored drink mix
1½ cups instant tea (you might use decaffeinated tea)
2 packages dry lemonade mix (1-quart size)
1 teaspoon ground cinnamon
¼ teaspoon ground cloves

Mix all ingredients well. Store in a jar or other moisture-proof container. Mix 3 teaspoons of tea powder in a cup of hot water.

2. Collect the students' papers and compile them into a booklet entitled "Recipes for Tear-Water Tea." Make the booklet available for free-time reading.

Evaluation

Make sure students have listed complete and appropriate ideas on their papers. Praise their efforts.

Variation

Have students work in small groups to generate ideas. This would be particularly helpful for ESL students who might need help articulating their ideas.

Tear-Water Tea

I could fill a teacup with tears if:

_____

_____

_____

_____

_____

_____

_____

Beginning Definitions

Objectives

Students will:
1. List ten items that have special significance.
2. Write a sentence to explain why each item is special.

Materials

A Hole Is to Dig, by Ruth Krauss
children's dictionary
lined paper
poster board
felt-tipped marker
pencils

Stimulus

1. Begin this lesson by having each student list ten things that are very special to them. These can be food items, activities, toys, games, places, or anything that has special significance. Make your own list while the students are writing.
2. Explain that a definition gives the purpose of a word and then gives examples for that word. Read sample definitions from the dictionary. For example: "A *toy* is an object that children play with; a doll, a stuffed animal."
3. Read *A Hole Is to Dig* aloud to the class. Explain that this book is filled with definitions. Ask if anyone has noted (on their lists of special things) any of the items mentioned in this book.

Activity

Give each student a sheet of lined paper. Ask the students to define each item on their lists of special things, imitating Ruth Krauss's pattern of defining words. Students should indicate in their definitions why these items are special to them. They may give more than one definition for each word, just as Ruth Krauss does. Be sure to write definitions for your special things, too.

Follow-up

1. Over the next several days, have students volunteer to read their lists and definitions.
2. Display the definitions on a bulletin board. Make a master list on poster board of items that several different students include on their individual lists. Write all the definitions of these words. Point out how differently some words are defined.

Evaluation

Note the clarity of students' definitions. Comment on those definitions that are general enough to serve for various situations, but specific enough to be meaningful.

Objectives

Students will:
1. Create metaphors for colors.
2. Collectively write a sensory poem about the color red.
3. Write their own poems about a color.

Materials

items of various colors that students can smell, feel, taste, and/or hear (flowers, toys, fruit, vegetables, familiar insects, cornmeal, and so on)
bags
Hailstones and Halibut Bones, by Mary O'Neill
"Color Poems" activity sheet (p. 51)
"Color Poems" student examples (p. 52)
lined paper
crayons or felt-tipped pens
pencils

Stimulus

1. Collect objects of different colors that students can see, smell, feel, taste, or hear. Choose objects that seem representative of certain colors, if possible. Put each item in its own bag, and pass the bags around so that each student can smell, feel, taste, or listen to the object.
2. Read aloud the poem "Red" from *Hailstones and Halibut Bones*. Read other color poems from the book, too, if you wish.
3. Discuss how certain colors make people feel or what images they bring to mind.

Activity

1. Ask students for their sensory reactions to the color red. Record their responses on the chalkboard. Then, with the class, compose a sensory poem about the color red. Begin by exploring each sense: "Red is the taste of . . . , Red is the smell of . . . ," and so on. Then alter the poem as you and the students wish. Note that students are creating metaphors.
2. Give each student a copy of the activity sheet, a copy of the student examples, and a sheet of lined paper. Have students complete the activity sheet to get started and then write their own color poems about any color they

choose. They may use the student examples as models. Students should write their poems on lined paper.

Follow-up

Have students illustrate their poems. Make a "Color Poems" bulletin board display. Exhibit the poems with strips of colored construction paper on the bulletin board.

Evaluation

Observe student participation during the writing of the group poem. Read the completed poems, noting the detail of sensory descriptions and the creativity in the responses to certain colors. Make sure each poem is about one color only.

Variation

Check out the film *Hailstones and Halibut Bones* (Sterling) through your school district's media library or through a county library. Show this film instead of reading excerpts from the book.

Color Poems

Choose a color to write about. Complete each
sentence for that color. You may write more than one
response for some senses.

_____ is the taste of _____

_____

_____ is the smell of _____

_____

_____ is the feel of _____

_____

_____ is the sound of _____

_____

_____ is the sight of _____

_____

Now write a poem about this color. Include some of
the sensory responses listed above. Write your poem
on another sheet of paper, and save room to illustrate it.

Color Poems

Green is slime in a swamp.
Green is a ghost in a cemetery.
Green is grass and leaves on a tree.
Green is moss growing up a tree.
Green is a dragonfly flying in the air.
Green is the sea when it's rough.
Green makes me feel happy.
                    —*Morgan*

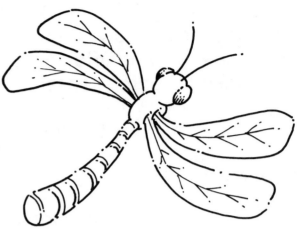

My favorite color is yellow, lovely,
You can see it in the sun.
Bananas, yummy, yum, muffins, pears.
A fire engine's yellow.
Autumn leaves. I love it—yellow!
                    —*Stephanie*

Red is the taste of underripe blackberries waiting to pucker in
    your mouth.
It's the taste of too-hot cocoa that burns all the way down to
    your stomach.
Red is the smell of autumn leaves burning.
It's the smell of a bonfire crackling on a summer night.
                    —*Lisa*

Homonym Happiness

Objectives

Students will:
1. Define a homonym.
2. Use homonyms in a story.

Materials

A Chocolate Moose for Dinner, by Fred Gwynne, *The King Who Rained*, also by Fred Gwynne, or another book that explores homonyms
lined paper
poster board
felt-tipped marker

Stimulus

1. Explain that a homonym is a word that is pronounced the same as another word that is spelled differently and has a different meaning (for example, *bare* and *bear* or *beat* and *beet*). Write the words "mousse" and "moose" on the chalkboard. Ask the students if they know what "mousse" means. (Explain that *mousse* is a pudding in French, if they don't know.) Then ask them to explain the word "moose." Be sure to point out that the words are pronounced the same.
2. Remind the students about homonyms they have come across in their reading texts. Make a list of examples students know.
3. Read *A Chocolate Moose for Dinner* aloud. Ask your students to list the homonyms they hear in the story. Explain, if necessary, that the author has used homonyms to have fun with words.
4. Divide the class into small groups and have the students list as many pairs of homonyms as they can in ten minutes. Compile a class list of different homonyms on the chalkboard or a large sheet of paper mounted on the wall.

Activity

Give each student a sheet of lined paper. Have each student write a homonym story similar to Fred Gwynne's. They should refer to the homonym list. Suggest that students brainstorm ideas for a story line first. Also suggest that they write titles that include homonyms.

Follow-up

1. Allow time for the students to illustrate their stories. Encourage them to read their stories aloud to the class and to have the other students list homonyms they hear.
2. Add to the group's list of homonyms. Discuss any homonyms the students don't understand. Make a permanent homonym chart, listing the students' words on poster board for reference.
3. As a homework assignment, have students write five sentences using some of the homonyms listed on the chart.

Evaluation

Scan the stories to make sure students understand what a homonym is, and to make sure they use homonyms correctly.

Worth a Thousand Words

Collect several wordless books from the library. *Pancakes for Breakfast,* by Tomie de Paola is an especially good book to use. Ask the students to be perfectly quiet as you present each page of the book. Together with the class, write a story to go with the book. First, try writing the story without referring to the pictures again, attempting to write text to correspond with each picture. Match the text to the picture story and fill in any story parts that appear to be missing. Clip a copy of the class-written story to the back of the wordless book for others to enjoy.

After modeling the process, encourage students to repeat the activity on their own for other wordless books. They may work individually or with a partner. Invite them to share their written work with the class. One student may read the words while another student shows the corresponding picture in the book.

Memorable Characters

After you have read a story to the class, ask each student to select a favorite character from the story. (Some good books to use for this activity are *James and the Giant Peach,* by Roald Dahl; the "Ramona" books, by Beverly Cleary; *Stone Fox,* by John Gardiner; and *Indian in the Cupboard,* by Lynn Reid Banks.) Have the students write a diary entry from that character's point of view. The students will pretend they are the characters they've selected and will write about incidents from the story or from daily life. Have the students write three to five times a week for about three weeks. Allow students to make diary entries only during planned writing sessions; each writing session may last from five to seven minutes. Invite students to read aloud from their entries without naming the featured character. Ask the others in the class to identify the featured character.

Word Change

Type (double-spaced) a short story (one or two pages of text) for the class. Underline words or phrases at random. To model the activity, copy a few lines of the story, including the underlining, onto the chalkboard. Ask the students to suggest words they could use in place of the underlined words. Write a couple of alternatives above the existing words. As a group, decide if you want to use the words to change the meaning, or if you want to just substitute words that mean the same thing.

After modeling the process, give each student a copy of the short story and direct the students to continue writing an alternate word for each underlined word. When students have completed the assignment, encourage them to read their revised stories aloud. Here is an example:

> Once upon a time, a long time ago, three bears *lived* in a *lovely* little house in the woods. Papa Bear was a *very big* brown bear with a very deep voice. Mama Bear was a bit smaller and had a *softer* voice. Baby Bear was the *smallest* of all, and his voice was *squeaky.*

Story Writing

Story writing (narrative) can take many forms. Therefore, when you ask students to write a story, you must define what you mean for that particular task. For example, you might want students to write a personal narrative or to retell a favorite story in their own words. On the other hand, you might want students to write an original short story that has characters, setting, plot, main problem, and resolution. If so, you must first teach them how to include these parts in a composition.

Whatever you have in mind for the story-writing assignment, it is always helpful for young writers to follow a model. Even when students understand the assignment, it is comforting for them to be able to refer to an example from time to time as they write. It is also a good idea to have students practice writing collectively before they venture out on their own to create a piece of original writing. By working first together with the entire class and then in smaller groups to accomplish first drafts, students can try different ideas and techniques in a "safe" environment, developing the confidence necessary to attempt story writing on their own.

Let's begin the story at a farm in Iowa.

Let's call our main characters "Emma" and "George."

Let's see, what could be the main problem in the story?

A Story Map

Objectives

Students will:
1. Define the essential parts of a story.
2. Identify characters, setting, and plot in a familiar story.

Materials

poster board
felt-tipped pen
"The Blue Wool Mitten" story
 (p. 57)
"A Story Map" activity sheet
 (p. 58)
any version of the story "The Three Bears"
pencils

Stimulus

1. Discuss the parts of a story with your class. Ask the students to help you list every element they can think of that is an important part of a story. Write all of their responses on the chalkboard. Ask questions that lead them to suggest the essential elements, if necessary. Listen for signs of a broad understanding and recognition of the subject of discussion.
2. Write the following words on a poster-board chart: characters, setting, plot. Discuss what each means.
3. Read "The Three Bears" aloud to the class. Ask the students to think about the story "The Three Bears" (or any other familiar story) as you map each essential part of the story. Ask questions so you can determine the students' level of comprehension. Collectively prepare a map like the one on the activity sheet.

Activity

1. Read "The Blue Wool Mitten" aloud to the class. Encourage students to listen for the story elements listed on the chart.
2. Give each student a copy of the activity sheet. Ask the students to name the characters of the story and to list them on their activity sheets. Write the names of the characters on the chalkboard as they name them. Next, ask them about the setting. Ask if there is more than one setting. (Some may say that the

grandmother's house is one, the road is another, and the inside and outside of the mitten are each separate settings.) Then have students identify elements of the plot so they will be able to identify characters' goals, the problem to be overcome, and the resolution. Ask for a brief description of each event in the story. Direct students to list each item on their activity sheets as you write on the chalkboard. They do not need to write complete sentences.
3. Review the map of the story with the class.

Follow-up

1. Select other familiar stories, such as "The Three Billy Goats Gruff," "Little Red Riding Hood," and "The Three Little Pigs." Have students work in groups of three or four to complete a map for one of these stories. Each group should read the story aloud first. Have at least two groups "analyze" the same story so that the entire class can compare the work of different groups.
2. Have each student complete a map for a given story in the reading text as homework. Use the completed assignment as the basis for a class discussion about the story.

Evaluation

Observe student participation. Scan a set of one of the completed maps to be sure students understand the different parts of a story.

The Blue Wool Mitten

On the longest, coldest day of winter, a small boy was out in the forest collecting wood for the fireplace. He was staying at his grandma's house. As she sat in the house knitting a pair of bright red mittens, she said to him, "Collect as much wood as you can. The wind is cold and we will need to keep the fire blazing brightly."

The boy was gone all morning, loading twigs and branches on his sled. He was cold and tired by this time. As he placed the last few branches on his sled, he dropped one of his old blue mittens. He was in such a hurry to get back home that he didn't notice that the mitten had fallen on the road. He pulled his heavy sled back toward his grandma's house.

When the boy was out of sight, a little gray mouse came creeping through the woods. She was shivering with the cold, and her whiskers were covered with ice. She spied the mitten lying on the road and crawled inside it to keep warm.

A few moments later, a bullfrog came hopping along through the snow. He, too, was chilled to the bone. When he saw the mouse peering out of the mitten he asked if he could come in, too. "Certainly!" said the mouse. "There's plenty of room."

No sooner were the two of them settled when an old owl flew down from a tree. "Is there room for me, too, whoo, whoo, whoo?" hooted the old owl. The mouse, who was naturally afraid of the owl, agreed. "You'll have to mind your manners, though," she said.

The owl promised to be polite. He crept carefully into the snuggly mitten. The three of them were settling in nicely when a jackrabbit happened by and asked if he could come in, too.

"It's getting mighty crowded in here," said the frog, "but I guess we can make room for one more."

The animals moved a little closer together, and the jackrabbit joined them. Soon a fox came along, trotting through the snow. Without even asking, she popped right into the mitten, bringing her bushy tail right along with her.

Now, the animals were really crowded together. All their tails and paws and wings were jumbled up. About this time a big old timber wolf spied the mitten. He wanted to come in, too. "I don't know how you'll ever fit, but you may as well try," said the little gray mouse. Somehow, the timber wolf squeezed in with the other animals. They certainly were all toasty warm!

After a while, the animals heard a snorting sound. Who should they see but a wild boar who insisted on coming into the mitten! But the animals shouted, "Oh, no! There's no room for you!"

The boar didn't listen, though. The day was so cold, and he was freezing out in the snow. He squeezed and pushed and somehow made it into the mitten. As the animals were adjusting, a very cold, very large black bear peered into the mitten. "I want to come in, too," he said.

"There's no room for you in here," said all the animals.

"Just move over a bit," said the bear. "There's always room for one more!" He took a deep breath and pushed himself in.

About this time a little black ant came hobbling along. She was old and tired and very, very cold. When she saw the mitten she knew that it would be the perfect place to get warm again. She crawled over and put her tiny foot inside.

The mitten, stretched far beyond endurance, could take no more. There was a sudden loud POP! and the seams of the mitten ripped apart, scattering all the animals into the snow.

Just at this moment, the little boy noticed that one of his blue mittens was missing. He left his sled and ran back along the road, searching for the mitten. He looked all over, but all he could find were tiny bits of blue yarn scattered in the snow. He thought he saw a little mouse running into the woods with a patch of blue on her head, but he didn't really believe his eyes.

"Oh, well. Grandma is knitting me some new red mittens, and she probably has them ready by now," he said. The boy hurried back to the sled and pulled it home.

A Story Map

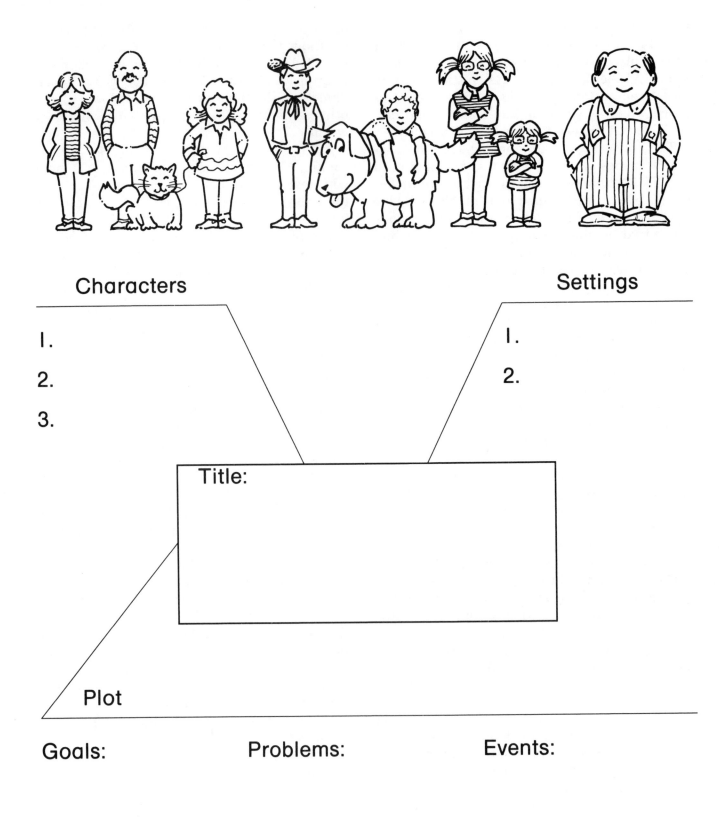

Characters

Settings

1.

2.

3.

1.

2.

Title:

Plot

Goals:

Problems:

Events:

Story ending:

Catching the Writing Express © 1987, David S. Lake Publishers

Progressive Stories

Objectives

Students will use what they know about the parts of a story to add to a story already begun.

Materials

"Progressive Stories" story starters (p. 60)
lined paper
timer

Stimulus

Quickly review the parts of a story (characters, setting, goals, problems, events, resolution) and list them on the chalkboard. Explain what will take place during the activity that follows.

Activity

1. Give each student a sheet of lined paper.
2. Write a story starter on the chalkboard (there are several listed on p. 60). Allow students enough time to copy the story starter onto paper. Then set the timer for three minutes; each student should begin writing a story based on the story starter, establishing the characters, setting, and goals.
3. When the timer signals, have each student draw a line across the page (directly under the last written line), write her or his name in the margin, and pass the paper to the student at the left.
4. Allow a minute or so for students to read what has already been written on the new papers they have just received. Then set the timer for three minutes and have the students add to the stories. Repeat this procedure seven more times. Announce the sixth

and seventh repetitions as the last two opportunities to add to the story. During the sixth repetition, students should include resolutions to the main problems; during the seventh repetition, students should write story endings.

Follow-up

1. Collect the stories and return each one to its originator. Divide the class into small groups of about five students. Have students read their stories aloud and compare the characters, settings, goals, problems, and events of each story in the group.
2. Have students revise and edit the stories they started writing, smoothing out style inconsistencies and any lapses in the story events.

Evaluation

Observe student participation. Collect the stories and read them. Make sure each story contains the essential parts. Praise the variety of characters and events in the different stories.

Progressive Stories

1. Sam opened his Bonus Burger to take out the onions and couldn't believe what he saw.

2. Marilyn was just getting ready to open her birthday gifts when suddenly the lights flickered and went out.

3. We had just gone inside the old haunted house and started up the stairs when we heard the front door slam shut.

4. Estella was sad about moving into a new apartment. Although the building she lived in now was old and tumbledown, it had been home for many years.

5. The Nguyens returned from a weekend vacation to find their yard in a disastrous state.

6. I wanted to grow a giant sunflower, but I had no idea it would be like this!

7. Thomas entered the science fair. His secret experiment was bound to stun the judges.

8. My sister and I have never gotten along very well, but this was our worst disagreement ever.

9. Bret was traveling down the ski slope at about 30 miles an hour. Suddenly he realized he had strayed off the course.

10. The hot-air balloon began to rise, and I felt the basket leave the ground.

Pourquoi Stories

Objectives

Students will:
1. Define a *pourquoi* story.
2. List ideas for original *pourquoi* stories.
3. Write a *pourquoi* story.

Materials

A Story, A Story, by Gail E. Haley
Anansi the Spider: A Tale from the Ashanti, by Gerald McDermott
Why Mosquitoes Buzz in People's Ears: A West African Tale, by Verna Aardema
poster board
felt-tipped pen
lined paper
pencils

Stimulus

Extend this lesson over the course of a few days.

1. Read *A Story, A Story* aloud to the class. Explain that this story tells where stories come from. Ask questions such as the following to generate discussion about this story: "Why did they call Anansi 'the spider man'?" "Did the sky god think Anansi could pay the price of the stories?" "Why would someone write a story to explain where stories come from?"
2. Tell the class that a *pourquoi* story explains why something is the way it is. *Pourquoi* is the French word for "why."
3. On the following day, read *Anansi the Spider* aloud to the class and discuss the story with the class. Ask the students if this story is a *pourquoi* story, and ask what it explains.
4. Ask the students what other things *pourquoi* stories might explain. Make a list on poster board of their suggestions.
5. The next day, read *Why Mosquitoes Buzz in People's Ears* aloud to the class and discuss the story. Point out that *pourquoi* stories do not have to be real.

Activity

1. Divide the class into small groups. Display the poster-board list of story ideas. Have the groups discuss these and other story ideas.

Allow about ten minutes for each student to choose a story idea, discuss it with the group, and help others with story details.
2. Have students return to their desks and begin writing their stories. Remind students what they have learned about the parts of a story. (You may wish to have students chart the parts of their stories before writing. If so, give each student a copy of "A Story Map" on p. 58.) Allow two days for the writing stage. Give students an opportunity to meet in their small groups periodically to share ideas and to comment on progress made each day.

Follow-up

1. Have students meet in their groups to read their completed stories.
2. Regroup the students and have them read their stories aloud to their new audience.
3. Collect the stories and collate them in a class book.

Evaluation

Circulate during the writing stage to observe the process and to offer help when necessary. Sit in on the readings to hear a few of the completed stories. Read the stories to make sure each one meets the criteria of a *pourquoi* story.

Story Scripts

Objectives

Students will:
1. Determine setting, characters, and plot in a familiar story.
2. Collectively write a script based on a familiar story.

Materials

several scripts or plays from the library
poster board
felt-tipped pen
"The Lion and the Mouse" story (p. 63)
lined paper

Stimulus

1. Explain that a script needs all the parts of a story but that the format is different. Distribute the scripts or plays, and have the students pass them around so they can see what the script format looks like.
2. Discuss dialogue, narration, and stage directions. Have students look through the scripts or plays to find examples of each format item.
3. Read "The Lion and the Mouse" on p. 63.
4. Ask your students to identify the characters and to describe each one. Record their responses on the chalkboard. Next, ask students to identify the settings and to describe them. Again, record their responses on the chalkboard. Finally, ask them what happened in the story, in sequence. List the events briefly on the chalkboard, and explain that this is the plot.

Activity

Together with the class, make a script of "The Lion and the Mouse." Write it on the poster board. Begin writing the first few lines of the script as follows:

> Act I Scene I
> Setting: In the jungle. Trees, bushes, and rocks are around the stage. At stage right is a small meadow. A boar, two monkeys, and three zebras are standing among the trees. The lion enters left and walks to center stage.
> Lion (boastfully): I am the most handsome and powerful animal in the entire jungle.

Have students continue scripting the story, writing in small groups. (Act II naturally begins after the lion releases the mouse.)

Follow-up

1. When the class has finished scripting the story, select students to take the characters' parts, and have them act out the story, reading from the script. The others in the class can be critics, noting if anything is missing from the story or if changes in stage direction should be made. Make the suggested corrections to the script. Then have students copy the script onto lined paper.
2. Divide the class into several groups. Have each group act out the play for the class, either as a play or as a puppet show. Provide materials for students to make simple scenery and to make stick puppets or finger puppets if they wish.

Evaluation

Observe student participation during the scripting activity. As the groups present their renditions of the play, note how they handle dialogue, scenery, and dramatic expression.

Once upon a time a proud and handsome lion was roaming through the jungle, exclaiming how powerful he was and how happy everyone should be in the company of the king of beasts. After an afternoon of boasting, he became very sleepy. So he stretched out to take a nap in a peaceful meadow.

A small mouse, who made her home on the edge of the meadow, was scurrying back to her home after a day of hunting food. She was in such a rush to reach her snug little nest that she didn't even notice the lion. She ran right over his back and was on the top of his head when he awoke with a start. He immediately caught the mouse in his paws, saying, "How dare you wake *me*, the king of beasts! You will have to pay with your life. Besides, I'm hungry after my afteroon nap, and you will be a tasty morsel to eat." Then he opened his mouth, ready to devour the little mouse.

The mouse, who was worried about her children, wasn't ready to be eaten. So she pleaded with the lion. "Oh, King of Beasts, you are the greatest, most powerful animal in all the world. Please, show your mercy and spare me. I didn't mean to wake you. I was only hurrying to feed my babies. Besides, there may come a time when I can repay the favor and save your life."

The lion, who was getting bored with the first part of the mouse's speech, was overcome with laughter when the mouse said she might repay the favor. "You! Save me? Preposterous!" He laughed until tears came to his eyes. "No, I don't think you'll ever be able to save me. But because you have told me such a good joke I'll let you go. Just be sure not to bother me again."

The mouse, feeling very relieved, quickly scampered home.

Weeks passed and all was quiet in the jungle until one day the sound of guns could be heard. Most of the animals trembled and hid—but not the lion. He continued roaming through the forest, showing how brave and fearless he was. Suddenly he began roaring in anger and frustration. He'd stepped into a hunter's net and was now hanging upside down from a large tree. He was absolutely helpless.

The mouse heard the angry roars of the lion. She quickly investigated to see if she could repay her debt to the lion. As soon as she saw the problem, she climbed the tree, crawled along the main branch, and began to gnaw on the rope that was holding the lion. Soon, the net was opened and the lion bounced down to the ground, bumping his nose as he landed. He was very grateful to be free. "Indeed, you are a brave little mouse. Your debt to me is repaid in full. No longer shall I make fun of such a little creature. It appears that size isn't all that counts in the jungle." The lion walked off into the jungle, this time carefully watching where he was stepping.

Comic Strip Dialogue

Select several newspaper comic strips that tell a continuing story. Collect the strips for about ten days. Arrange each set of strips sequentially, and make a copy of the original. Then cut out (or white out) the dialogue and make a copy—enlarged, if possible. Also make a transparency of one set of strips so you can model the writing activity for the class.

Display the transparency on an overhead projector, covering up all but the first comic strip in the series. Ask students to study the frames and to suggest dialogue for each balloon, using the picture context as a guide. Show the next strip and continue filling in the dialogue balloons, using student suggestions. Remind the students that these strips tell a continuing story. After completing all the strips on the transparency, read the dialogue carefully. Invite students to suggest changes. When the class is satisfied with its version of the comic strip, read the original comic strip and compare the story lines.

Give each student a copy of another set of blank-balloon comic strips you prepared. Have the students fill in dialogue to create story lines on their own. Give them an opportunity to share their comic strips with one another and to compare their comic strips with the originals.

Science Writing

With the class, research the life cycle of an animal such as the butterfly or frog. Read several books, both fiction and nonfiction, on the topic. (If you choose the topic of butterflies, consider beginning the activity by reading *The Very Hungry Caterpillar*, by Eric Carle.) Then have each student explain, in writing, the life cycle of that animal. The student should use one page to describe and to illustrate each stage of development. Emphasize the sequence of development.

This activity reinforces sequential development. It also demonstrates that stories are all around us, just waiting to be written. Repeat the activity using other topics, such as the development of any plant or animal.

A Surprise Gift

Fill a box with an appropriate treat for the class, such as unpopped popcorn, erasers, or sugarless gum. Wrap the box with fancy gift wrap (not birthday or seasonal wrapping paper) and a ribbon. Put the gift box on a table in front of the class, and ask the students to visualize what is inside the box. Let them brainstorm. If they have trouble getting started, make some suggestions or ask questions.

Ask them to write a story about how the box came to be in their classroom. Have them begin the story "Once upon a time . . ." so they have the sense that you want a real story. Each story should include a character who is giving the gift and a character who is receiving the gift. Ask them to reveal what might be in the box. Invite students to read their stories aloud. Then open the box and share the treat.

What I Know About

The lessons in this unit offer students an opportunity to practice writing compositions about themselves—about who they are, what they can do, and what they know. These lessons are all exercises in expository writing. They require the student to explain facts and to relate information in a logical, organized fashion.

Children learn a great deal at school and at home. They learn how to ride bicycles, how to alphabetize, how to multiply numbers, how to make snacks for themselves, how to locate books in the library. They learn many things that they can write about. All of these skills make excellent topics for expository compositions.

In these lessons, students will apply some of the writing skills they already have, such as developing an idea into an organized paragraph. These lessons challenge students' logical thinking skills. In addition, they help students realize that the purpose of writing is to communicate a meaningful idea.

Writing Directions

Objectives

Students will:
1. List all the ingredients and utensils needed to make a peanut butter and jelly sandwich.
2. Write step-by-step directions for making a sandwich.

Materials

lined paper
whole wheat bread (about five loaves)
peanut butter (several small jars)
no-sugar fruit spread (several jars)
plastic knives
paper plates
cutting board
sandwich bags
sponge
pencils

Stimulus

Before you begin this lesson, you may wish to contact students' parents and ask for help in supplying the materials. Do not display the materials for the class to see.

Ask the class, "Who knows how to make a peanut butter and jelly sandwich?" Then ask what utensils they would need to make such a sandwich. Record *all* of their responses on the chalkboard. Next, ask what ingredients they would need. Again, list the items they mention. Discuss this list.

Activity

1. Give each student a sheet of lined paper. Tell the students to think carefully about how to make a peanut butter and jelly sandwich. Instruct them to write step-by-step directions, in sequence, for mkaing the sandwich. Students should work independently and should not consult each other. They may include drawings to illustrate the procedure. Explain that someone must be able to follow their directions *exactly* to complete the task. Allow about fifteen minutes for students to complete the assignment.
2. Collect the papers and distribute them, making sure that no one receives her or his own paper.

3. Divide the class into small groups, and have each student choose a partner within that group. Have each group collect the materials they will need to set up a working area in the classroom. (The group can share a jar of peanut butter and a jar of fruit spread.)
4. Each student will make a sandwich according to the directions that the partner reads aloud. The students must follow the directions exactly as they are written.
5. Make sure students clean up and put away materials.

Follow-up

Collect the students' directions. Discuss the lesson. Ask if anyone had difficulty following the written directions. Encourage students to describe their experiences. Ask if they can think of a way to rewrite the directions so they are easier to follow. Record their ideas on the chalkboard. Return the students' papers and invite them to revise their directions.

Evaluation

Note the sequence and detail of the sandwich-making directions. Compare the students' first set of directions with their revised directions.

Blooming

Objectives

Students will:
1. List skills they already have and others they look forward to acquiring.
2. Write a paragraph about one skill from each category.

Materials

Leo the Late Bloomer, by Robert Kraus
lined paper
"Blooming" activity sheet (p. 68)
pencils

Stimulus

1. Lead a discussion about how children grow. Point out how helpless babies are but how quickly they learn to crawl, walk, talk, and so on. Explain that this kind of growth continues throughout life. Ask students to describe how it feels to master a new skill or to learn new ideas. Share how you felt about something new you learned recently.
2. Ask what kinds of things students would like to learn at school or at home. Share with them some things you'd like to learn or some skill you'd like to improve.
3. Read *Leo the Late Bloomer* aloud to the class. Ask students how Leo felt when he couldn't do anything, and how he felt at the end of the story.

Activity

1. Give each student a sheet of lined paper. Direct students to list at least five things they expect to be able to do one day but cannot do yet. These can be skills they are learning now (such as using a computer or passing a timed math facts test), or accomplishments they hope to achieve (such as speaking a foreign language). They can even be privileges they hope to receive (such as staying up till midnight).
2. Then ask students to list five things they can do now that they couldn't do when they were in kindergarten. These can be skills they learned at home or at school (such as riding a bicycle), or privileges they have earned (such as walking to school by themselves).

3. Now ask students to read their lists and draw a star next to the most important item on each list. They should think carefully about each choice.
4. Give each student a copy of the activity sheet. Ask students to write a paragraph about each of the starred items on their lists. The paragraphs should explain how the students feel about those skills or privileges.

Follow-up

1. Divide the class into small groups and have students share their paragraphs.
2. Encourage students to seek out other class members who have similar goals, comparing the lists they wrote.
3. Make a class book that records the accomplishments of the students, taken from their lists.

Evaluation

Circulate around the classroom to help students as needed with their writing. Encourage them to develop their thoughts in an organized fashion. Collect the activity sheets. Praise students' accomplishments and their desire to learn something new. Note if you can help students with any skills they wish to acquire.

Complete the sentence below. Write a paragraph telling about a skill or a privilege you wish to gain.

Example:
    I have not yet "bloomed" at skiing downhill.

I have not yet "bloomed" at _____

_____

_____

_____

_____

Now write a paragraph about a skill or privilege you do have.

I have "bloomed" at _____

_____

_____

_____

_____

_____

Catching the Writing Express © 1987, David S. Lake Publishers

Meet My Family

Objectives

Students will:
1. Write a brief description of each person in their families.
2. Assemble a family portrait book according to instructions.

Materials

"Meet My Family" directions for a portrait book (pp. 70-71)

12″ × 18″ sheets of construction paper

3″ × 14″ strips of construction paper

manila, pink, and brown construction paper with 2″ circles traced in pencil (as many circles as will fit)

scissors

crayons or felt-tipped pens

yarn (yellow, brown, orange, black, and gray)

glue

4½″ × 12″ lined paper

4½″ × 12″ construction paper

stapler

pencils

Stimulus

Before you begin the lesson, make a family portrait book according to the directions on pp. 70-71.

1. If possible, bring a real family portrait to class. Name each person in the picture and briefly tell your class about each person. Invite students to tell about their families. Point out that each person looks and acts differently from everyone else in the family and that each person has different responsibilities. Ask students to tell what their responsibilities are at home. Then ask them to think about the responsibilities of each person in their families.
2. Show the class your model family portrait book. Point out how each person looks different.

Activity

1. Have each student list the members of his or her family and write a couple of interesting and important things about each person. (If a student is an only child, she or he may include grandparents and/or favorite aunts and uncles in the family portrait.)

2. Have each student write a composition about her or his family, based on the descriptions and notes made. The composition should be written on sheets of lined paper, 4½″ × 12″, with lines running across the 12″ width.
3. Give each student a copy of the "Meet My Family" portrait book directions (both pages). Provide materials and have students follow the directions to complete the portrait book.

Follow-up

Allow time for students to view one another's portrait books. Invite students to read their family descriptions aloud. Display these projects on students' desks during Open House.

Evaluation

Observe student participation. Offer help with the portrait book directions if necessary. Make sure students have included a description of each family member pictured.

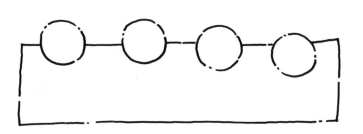

1. Cut a 2" circle for each member of your family.

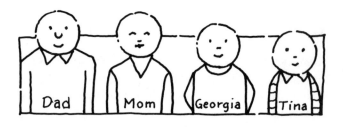

2. Glue the circles on a strip of 3" × 14" construction paper.

3. Draw the face and upper body of each person. Remember to make each one different.

4. Glue on yarn for hair. Write each person's name.

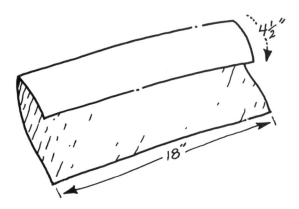

5. Fold a sheet of 12" × 18" construction paper as shown.

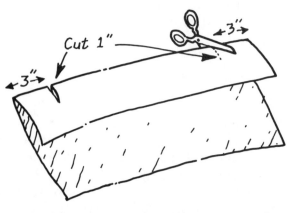

6. Make a 1" deep cut on the fold, 3" from each side.

Catching the Writing Express © 1987, David S. Lake Publishers

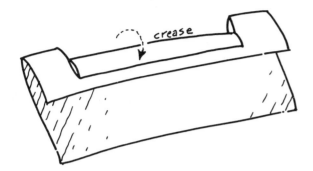

7. Fold and crease.

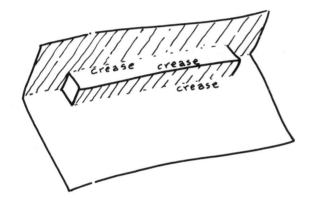

8. Open the paper and push the creased section to the other side.

9. Glue your family strip onto the creased section, keeping the creased section open.

Meet the Simms Family

10. Make a book cover on 4½" × 12" construction paper.

11. Place the book cover on top of your composition describing your family. Staple the cover and your composition opposite the family portrait.

Catching the Writing Express © 1987, David S. Lake Publishers

When I Grow Up

Objectives

Students will:
1. Write a three-paragraph essay about their future plans.
2. Use transitions to organize the essay paragraphs.

Materials

"When I Grow Up" activity sheet (p. 73)
pencils

Stimulus

1. Begin by telling the class what career you had hoped to follow when you were young. Point out how you followed your career plan or veered from it to find a different plan. Ask your students what they currently plan to be when they grow up. Let students briefly tell what careers they hope to follow and why.
2. Explain that a *transition* is a bridge between two thoughts. A transition links the different thoughts with some point of similarity. It makes paragraphs flow smoothly. Use your discussion of career plans to exemplify a transition. Explain that sometimes a transition is just a linking word, such as "therefore" or "however." Sometimes, though, we need a whole sentence that provides a link between two ideas or thoughts. Point out that there is usually a transition word or sentence at the end or at the beginning of a new paragraph. Give examples.

Activity

Give each student a copy of the activity sheet. Discuss the directions and answer any questions the students may have. Direct the students to complete their essays independently.

Follow-up

1. Divide the class into small groups and have the students read their essays aloud to one another. Have the students comment on one another's essays, considering the points mentioned on the activity sheet, and suggest ways to improve the essays.
2. As a homework assignment, have each student revise the essay.

Evaluation

Collect both versions of the essays. Note the use of transition words and sentences; note whether the revision improved the essay. Praise students for their writing efforts, for supporting their classmates' efforts, and for attempting to improve their writing.

When I Grow Up

What plans do you have for your future? Tell about your job plans or other plans you have.

In your first paragraph, tell what led up to this plan. In your second paragraph, give the details of your plan. In the third paragraph, tell what you will have to do to achieve your goals. Be sure to write transition words and sentences to make your paragraphs flow smoothly.

_____

_____

_____

_____

_____

_____

_____

_____

_____

_____

_____

_____

_____

_____

_____

_____

Paragraph Pattern

Objectives

Students will:
1. Name specific topics based on general ones.
2. Review the pattern for writing an expository paragraph.
3. Write a paragraph using this pattern.

Materials

butcher paper
felt-tipped pen
"Paragraph Pattern" checklist (p. 75)
lined paper
pencils

Stimulus

1. Prepare a list of at least eight general topics that would be of interest to your class. These may be related to anything in the curriculum or to personal interests expressed by your students. Topics could include pets, homework, foods, math, science, or communities. Write the topics on the left side of a large sheet of butcher paper that you have folded vertically into thirds.
2. Ask the student to help you list specific topics from the list of general topics. For example, the topics "dogs," "cats," and "fish," are more specific than the general topic "pets." Try to get the students to narrow the topic even more. For example, ask them what would be more specific than the topic "dogs" ("beagle" is one topic that is more specific than "dogs").
3. Continue through the list of general topics, having students suggest related specific topics.
4. Give each student a copy of the checklist. Read it together.
5. Choose one of the specific topics. Write a paragraph about this topic, asking students to help you. Write the sentences according to the checklist pattern.

Activity

Have each student choose a specific topic and write a paragraph, referring to the checklist as needed.

Follow-up

Have students read their paragraphs in pairs or in small groups. Invite volunteers to read their paragraphs to the entire class.

Evaluation

Read each paragraph to make sure students understand the elements of a good paragraph. Select several paragraphs to be used as models of good paragraph form, and display these in the classroom. Try to rotate the models.

Paragraph Pattern

Checklist Items	Examples
1. Choose a topic that is specific.	"My Mutt"
2. State a point of view, an idea, or an opinion about the topic.	"My mutt, Perky, is an extremely friendly dog."
3. Support your statement with at least three reasons.	"Perky wags his tail all the time. He licks all visitors, including the mail carrier. When my friends come over, he cries to be let into the house."
4. Restate the main idea in a different way.	"Sometimes I wish that Perky weren't quite so friendly."

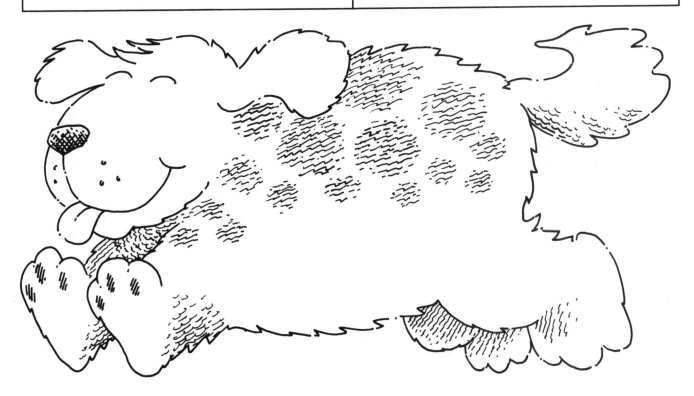

Compare and Contrast

Bring a raw potato and an apple to class. Pass them around so each student may inspect them closely. Cut each one in half and show the insides.

Draw three columns on the chalkboard. Label them, in order from left to right, "Apple," "Same," and "Potato." Ask the students to tell you what the apple and the potato have in common. They might suggest that both of these objects grow, that they have a roundish shape, that they weigh about the same, or that both objects are white inside. Record their responses in the middle column.

Next, hold up the apple pieces and ask them to tell you about it. Each response should only suit the apple and not the potato. (For example, the response "It is sweet" might suit the apple but not the potato, whereas the response "It is juicy" would suit either object.) Ask the students to tell you about the potato. Again, question their responses to make sure they really think the descriptions are only suitable for the potato. Some responses really cause students to think. For example, the response "You eat it cooked" is suitable for both objects, but students may initially think it only suitable for the potato. In such an instance, remind them about baked apples or apple pie, and guide them to recategorize the response. Record each response in the correct column.

Repeat this thinking activity with several other objects or topics, such as the sun and the moon, a dog and a cat, lunch and breakfast. Ask students to suggest items to compare and contrast. Have the students repeat this thinking activity individually and share their lists with the class. Assign the activity as homework, and have students involve their families. Later, have the students write a paragraph about each category of data collected.

A Process Journal

Plan a seed-planting experiment in your class, and have each student keep a plant-growth journal. Collect several different kinds of seeds, or ask students to bring seeds to class. Planting popcorn kernels or dried beans is usually quite sucessful. Wheat kernels, mung beans, or alfalfa seeds grow quickly and yield edible plants.

Gather enough containers (such as small milk cartons or large seedling pots) so that each student has one. You will also need some potting soil and a tray in which to keep the planting containers. Have each student select and plant a few of the same kind of seed and then label his or her container with name, variety of seeds, and planting date. After planting, moisten the soil and cover the containers with plastic wrap to retain moisture.

Have each student make a journal in which to keep a running record of the plant's growth. The first entry of the journal should list the variety of seeds and the date they were planted. Students should describe the process they went through to select the seed variety, to plant the seeds, and to care for them. Direct students to make entries daily, even though they won't see much happen during the first few days.

Show students how to carefully remove the top soil every few days so they can see the size of their seeds change and the roots begin to develop. Once the seeds sprout, have students measure the daily growth and record it. Encourage them to examine the leaves carefully to see which are the sprouting leaves and which are true leaves.

Suggest that students include illustrations and a growth graph in their journals. If you continue this project for three weeks, students will learn much about describing their observations. This activity demonstrates that writing is important in science.

Growing As a Writer

What is good writing? How do we teach students to identify their best efforts? Revising or editing is an important part of good writing. We should teach students that we don't expect perfection the first time around; a composition takes time and careful thought.

Writing begins with a rough draft, a way of getting thoughts down on paper in the approximate form desired. To facilitate the revision step, students should write their rough drafts using every other line of a sheet of lined paper. Remind them to leave wide margins for changes, additions, and notes.

Provide examples of your own marked-up rough drafts. It will help students get accustomed to revising their compositions if they see examples. They also need to see that the teacher doesn't always get it right the first time, either! In addition, if you use the dictionary and a thesaurus frequently when you are editing, students will realize that you consider these books necessary tools.

Chart the steps of the revision process, and model all the steps as you discuss them with the class. This unit contains a checklist entitled "Steps to Good Writing," which you may use. Students may suggest additional steps. If the suggested steps seem reasonable and helpful, add them to the list.

This unit contains three lessons especially designed to help students edit or revise their compositions. In these lessons, they will be editing their own writing as well as one another's work. These and other editing lessons you design will help students learn the qualities of effective writing.

Making a Writing Folder

Objectives

Students will:
1. Make folders in which to keep their writing.
2. Discuss steps to good writing.

Materials

legal-size manila folders
ruler
lined paper
stapler
felt-tipped pens
"Steps to Good Writing" checklist (p. 79)

Stimulus

1. Discuss the importance of organization to a writer. Explain that it is difficult to work on a composition if you cannot find it, or if it's all wrinkled because it was stuffed in the back of the desk. Also point out how valuable it is to have access to compositions written long ago to compare them with compositions currently being written.
2. Make a folder for each student as follows: Open a legal-size manila folder and fold up the bottom portion to make a 2½" flap. Crease the flap well, and close the folder.
3. Give each student a folder and tell the students that they now have a place to keep their compositions—those they've completed as well as those they are currently working on. Their compositions will remain in their folders for a full grading period so they will have the opportunity to revise or add to papers they've worked on in the past.

Activity

1. Have students write their names on the front of the folders and label the folders "Writing Folder."
2. Direct students to write "Work in Progress" on the inside left flap and "Completed Work" on the inside right flap. Each student may keep a sheet of lined paper labeled "Writing Ideas" under the inside left flap, and use this sheet to list ideas for writing topics. When the student has free writing time and can't think of a topic, he or she can check the list.

3. Ask each student to staple a sheet of lined paper to the outside back of the folder and write the heading "Completed Work." Students will record their completed compositions on this sheet, writing the title of the composition and the date completed.
4. Give each student a copy of the checklist. Discuss this checklist, have students suggest other steps that might be added to the list, and ask them to store it under the inside right flap of the folder. Students may keep another sheet of lined paper under this flap to record all the things they learn about writing, such as proofreading marks.
5. Have students decorate their writing folders.

Follow-up

Have students transfer all writing papers into their new folders. Allow time for them to copy titles of completed work and to list ideas for writing topics. Set up an easily accessible drawer or box to store the folders.

Evaluation

As students discuss the steps to good writing, note how much they have learned about writing. Check to see that students are using their folders to help them organize and keep track of their writing.

Steps to Good Writing

1. Write your first draft.

2. Read your work aloud. Listen to the sound of your words.

3. Have a partner read your work aloud.

4. Is the message clear? Does the composition say what you want it to? Which words could be changed to get your point across?

5. Read it to a group of friends. What is their response?

6. Remember that writing can be changed! Cross out words you want to change. Rewrite words above the line. Use a colored pencil if possible.

7. Check spelling. Use a dictionary.

8. Show your revised work to a partner, a group of friends, or your teacher. Is your message clear now? Make other changes if you wish.

9. Copy your writing on final-draft paper, making the changes you decide on.

Can you think of other steps to add to this list?

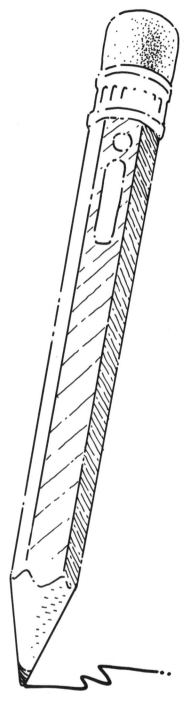

_____

_____

_____

Catching the Writing Express © 1987, David S. Lake Publishers

Editing a Story

Objectives

Students will:
1. Read a fable that contains mechanical errors.
2. Locate mechanical errors and correct them.
3. Add descriptive detail to a story.

Materials

any of Aesop's fables
"Editing a Story" activity sheet (p. 81)
lined paper

Stimulus

Read or tell a fable to the class. Aesop's fable "The Hare and the Tortoise" is a good one. Discuss the moral of the story. Ask the students to name the events in the story, telling how the story began, progressed, and ended.

Activity

Give each student a copy of the activity sheet. Read the directions aloud, and make sure the students understand them. Remind them that there are two tasks to complete: correcting the spelling, capitalization, and punctuation of the paragraph; crossing out words and making corrections above the line; and inserting descriptive words to make the paragraph more interesting. Urge students to accomplish each task separately and in order. Show students how to use a caret to note insertions. Have the students work independently to complete the assignment.

Follow-up

After students have had ample time to complete the assignment, have them compare their results. Read the fable, sentence by sentence, and point out the mechanical errors. Have the students count the errors they found and write the number at the bottom of the page. Discuss any discrepancies.

As you review this stage of the assignment, remember that even the mechanics of composition require flexibility. What one student sees as correct, another may see as incorrect—and both students *may* be right. (This is especially true when it comes to commas.) In addition, there is more than one way to correct an error. (For example, one student may add a conjunction to fix a run-on sentence, while another student may break the sentence into two separate sentences.)

Review the story. Ask students to read their revised sentences, noting the added words and phrases. Discuss their changes. Then have the students copy their revised stories on lined paper.

Evaluation

Have students pair up and read one another's revised fables, checking to see that the errors were corrected and that at least three descriptive words or phrases were added. Students may note whether the additions help to make the story more interesting.

Editing a Story

You are the editor at a publishing company. You want to publish this fable, but it is full of mistakes. Your job is to:

1. Find the mistakes and change them.
2. Add words to make the story more interesting.

The wind and the Son

Wunce upon a time when everything could talk, the Wind and the Sun fell into a a Argument about witch was stronger Finally they decided to putt the matter to a test, They would see which one could make a sertin man who was walking along the road throw off his cape. The Wind tried first He blue and he blue and he blue. The harder and colder he blew the tighter the traveler wrapped his cape around him at last the Wind gave up, saying, I give up Its your turn to try

The Sun begun to smile and as it grew warmer the traveler was comfortable once more. But the Sun shone brighter until the man grew hot, the swet poured down his face. he became tired. seating himself on a stone, he threw his cape on the ground

You see, gentleness had accomplished what force could not.

Checking on Our Writing

Objectives

Students will:
1. Review the definition of a *pourquoi* story.
2. Write a *pourquoi* story.
3. Evaluate each other's writing using a checklist.

Materials

The Elephant's Child, by Rudyard Kipling
"Checking on Our Writing" activity sheet (p. 83)
lined paper
pencils

Stimulus

This is a good follow-up lesson to the Unit 5 lesson "*Pourquoi* Stories." Ask students to define the term "*pourquoi* story." Students may use the term "why story" instead.

Read *The Elephant's Child* aloud to the class. Discuss the story. List the characteristics of this type of story. Ask the students to identify the parts of the story.

Activity

1. Give each student a copy of the activity sheet, which lists the characteristics of a *pourquoi* story. Although students will not be using this form until the follow-up activity, it may be a useful reference.
2. Have students brainstorm a list of ideas for *pourquoi* tales. Examples: why the seasons change, why the sky is blue, or why penguins can't fly.
3. Ask each student to choose an idea and write an original tale on lined paper.

Follow-up

Divide the class into groups of four or five students. Read the directions on the activity sheet with the students. Have students read their stories aloud to the group members. The students will score each story after it is read, marking the score on the activity sheet.

Evaluation

Students are evaluating each other's (and their own) writing in small groups. Circulate around the classroom and note how the editing process is working out.

Checking on Our Writing

A *pourquoi* story explains why something is the way it is. Like any good story, it has a beginning, a middle, and an end.

Write the name of each group member. Take turns reading your stories. Give a score for each story. Score on five items. For each item, give a score of 1, 2, or 3. The best score is 3. Then total the scores for each story. The best total score is 15.

Group Member

Item:				
1. What the story explains (the topic of the story)				
2. How the story begins				
3. How the story progresses (the middle of the story)				
4. How the story ends				
5. The description in the story				
TOTAL SCORE				

In your group, talk about the scores you give each story. Try to agree on the scores.

Editing a Partner's Writing

Objectives

Students will:
1. Review the steps of good writing.
2. Collectively edit a student's composition.
3. Edit a partner's composition on their own.

Materials

rough draft of a student's composition
overhead projector
"Editing a Partner's Writing" activity sheet (p. 85)
colored pencils
lined paper

Stimulus

Select a rough draft of a composition to use for demonstration. Choose a composition that is written on every other line of a sheet of lined paper. Make a transparency of the page. Using an overhead projector, display the rough draft for the class to see.

Read the selection aloud. Begin by discussing the good points of the composition. Have students volunteer comments and support them with examples. Discuss changes that would make the composition better. Model how to make those changes. Make the changes in between the lines and in a different color ink. Ask students to suggest changes they think would improve the paper.

Students often suggest improvements by asking questions. For example, instead of stating that the description should have more detail, a student might ask what a certain character looks like. Instead of stating that the sequence of events is confusing, a student might ask, "Why did this happen first?" or "Why did the story end so quickly?" Help the students translate their questions into helpful suggestions. Ask how they might rewrite or add to the story to make it better. Rewrite the story with the students' help.

Activity

1. Give each student a copy of the activity sheet.
2. Direct the students to locate the rough draft papers from their last writing assignment and have the papers handy.

3. Review the steps of good writing. Remind them what they will be looking for in a composition as they edit it.
4. Have each student choose a partner to work with. Each person will read the partner's rough draft and edit it as you had shown, writing comments on the activity sheet first and then editing directly on the rough draft using a colored pencil. Encourage students to list at least one positive comment on the worksheet.

Follow-up

1. Allow time for the students to review their partner's comments and changes. Then bring the group back together. Ask the students how they felt about receiving help. If you repeat the activity frequently, it will become easier for students to accept the comments and they will benefit more from it each time.
2. Give students an opportunity to rewrite their compositions based on the partner's comments and changes.

Evaluation

Check the students' rough drafts, activity sheets, and rewrites to see if they have a clear picture of the revision process. Praise their improvement. Make sure students are attempting to be helpful with the comments they give one another.

Editing and Revising Worksheet

Editor: _____ Date: _____

Title of composition: _____

Author of composition: _____

Suggestions: _____

_____

_____

_____

_____

_____

_____

_____

_____

_____

_____

_____

_____

_____

_____

Correcting Mechanical Errors

Think of areas of writing in which your students need practice. Write a short story for your students to edit, including a few mechanical errors to be corrected in each area. Write a corrected version of the story so that students can check their editing.

Demonstrate the use of proofreading symbols. Make a copy of the uncorrected story for each student. As you distribute the story, explain that you wrote the story for them and that you think it's pretty good but that, since you wrote it quickly, it might have a few mistakes. Challenge them to find all the mistakes. If possible, have the students use colored pencils for their editing.

Students as Editors

Try this activity when your students have had some practice writing sentences and correcting them. Have each student write three sentences, each containing four mistakes (writing on every other line on lined paper). Have the students pair up and exchange papers. Direct the partners to underline the errors using a bright-colored crayon. Then the partners will copy each sentence, correcting the errors. When they have completed their editing, have students exchange papers again so that they have their own papers. The students can then check to see that all intentional errors were found and corrected. The students may be surprised to see that some unintentional errors were spotted by their partners!

Learning to Revise

As you read though your students' compositions, collect sentences that exemplify unclear writing. Copy or type these, without identifying the writer, onto a duplicating master, leaving some ample space between lines. Have the students rewrite the sentences more clearly. Encourage students to share their answers and also to share their feelings about reading the unclear sentences. After your students have demonstrated an understanding of revising for clarity, assign additional sentences as homework.

Discovering the Importance of Word Order

Write a fairly long sentence on the chalkboard, but scramble the words as you write. For example, "On the first day of school my bus was fifteen minutes late, so I was late for class" might look like "day school was so my late, On bus I class minutes for fifteen the first was late of." (Begin with a shorter sentence for second graders.)

Challenge the students to unscramble the sentence. Tell them that they must use every word and that they cannot add words. Allow about five minutes. If the students are really puzzled, work out the first five words with them. Remind them to look for clues such as capital letters or commas.

When time is up, have students volunteer to read their unscrambled sentences. Accept sentences that are different from your original but that still make sense. When everyone has had a chance to share, write your original sentence on the chalkboard under the scrambled sentence.

This book provides you with a nucleus for a strong writing program that will carry you and your student through the school year. On the following pages, you will find the Lesson Generator, which lists ideas to help you create more exciting writing lessons to supplement the ones in this book.

First, select any stimulus listed in column one. The stimuli are grouped in the following categories: short stories, films, children's books, poetry, and art. The stimulus may be considered a prewriting activity.

Then, from column two, decide on the type of main activity you want students to experience. The main activity is almost always a writing activity. It may also be an oral activity that supports the goals of the writing program.

In column three, we offer suggestions for following up a main activity. This column lists various ways of having students develop their writing. Finally, column four suggests evaluation techniques you may wish to try.

The wonderful thing about the Lesson Generator is that it encourages you to keep adding to the list. For example, you probably know of other stories and short books you can use to stimulate writing. Also, you may think of other categories of stimuli, such as field trips or observing objects. Keep jotting notes on this chart to remind you of interesting possibilities. You, too, can create SAFE lessons!

Stimulus

Short Stories

"Zlateh, the Goat", by Isaac Singer

"The Doughnuts", by Roger McCloskey

Petronella, by Jay Williams

Films

Rainshower
Churchill

String Bean
McGraw-Hill

Children's Books

I Love My Mother, by Paul Zindel

How to Go About Laying an Egg,
by Bernard Waber

Poetry

"Richard Cory", by E. A. Robinson

"Arithmetic", by Carl Sandburg

Where the Sidewalk Ends,
by Shel Silverstein

Art

Study a famous painting, sculpture,
or other piece of art.

ADD YOUR OWN IDEAS HERE.

Activity

Retell a story from different points of view.

Prepare a story for Readers' Theater.

Write poems using a word, syllable, or rhyme pattern.

Write poems based on literature.

Copy dialogue from a book.

Write dialogue for a wordless book or film.

Write a children's book.

Write a paragraph in the style of a given author.

Write a paragraph explaining what you like about a book.

Read folktales and select one for retelling.

Write an essay about a piece of art.

ADD YOUR OWN IDEAS HERE.

Follow-up

Share stories in small groups.

Read in pairs.

Illustrate reports.

Compile stories or poems into booklets.

Make a class "Big Book," compiling stories or poems by everyone in the class.

Create a school magazine.

Act out a dialogue.

Display student-written books at a book fair.

Tell stories to other classes.

Plan a Readers' Theater assembly.

Display essays on the bulletin board.

ADD YOUR OWN IDEAS HERE.

Evaluation

Teacher observation

Group evaluation according to criteria set by the class

Self-evaluation

Flow-chart questions

Student-teacher conferences

Cassette-taped readings

Editorial committee

Performance in front of a small group, the entire class, or other classes

Audience response

Proofreading

Holistic scoring

Analytical reading

Group discussion

ADD YOUR OWN IDEAS HERE.

Children's Books Cited in This Text

Unit 3

Lisker, Sonia. *I Used To.* Four Winds, 1977.

Unit 4

Shaw, Charles G. *It Looked Like Spilt Milk.* Harper, 1948.

Zolotow, Charlotte, *Summer Is . . .* Crowell, 1983.

Lobel, Arnold. "Tear-Water Tea." In *Owl at Home.* Harper, 1975.

Krauss, Ruth. *A Hole Is to Dig.* Harper, 1952.

O'Neill, Mary. *Hailstones and Halibut Bones.* Doubleday, 1961.

Gwynne, Fred. *A Chocolate Moose for Dinner.* Windmill, 1976.

Gwynne, Fred. *The King Who Rained.* Windmill, 1970.

de Paola, Tomie. *Pancakes for Breakfast.* Harcourt, 1978.

Dahl, Roald. *James and the Giant Peach.* Knopf, 1961.

Gardiner, John. *Stone Fox.* Crowell, 1980.

Banks, Lynn Reid. *Indian in the Cupboard.* Doubleday, 1981.

Unit 5

Haley, Gail. *A Story, A Story,* Atheneum, 1970.

McDermott, Gerald. *Anansi the Spider: A Tale from the Ashanti.* Holt, 1972.

Aardema, Verna. *Why Mosquitoes Buzz in People's Ears: A West African Tale.* Dial, 1975.

Carle, Eric. *The Very Hungry Caterpillar.* Putnam, 1981.

Unit 6

Kraus, Robert. *Leo the Late Bloomer.* Windmill, 1971.

Unit 7

Kipling Rudyard. *The Elephant's Child.* Walker, 1970.

Here is a list of good books to share with your students. Through reading aloud, you teach your students to read, to think, and to write. As they listen, students learn about:

- grammar
- writing style
- imagery and figurative language
- new ideas or new ways to express ideas
- the joy of a good book

Always have a good book going in your classroom. Plan time for the students to think about what the class has read together.

Bang, Molly. *Ten, Nine, Eight.* Greenwillow, 1983.

Bang, Molly. *The Grey Lady and the Strawberry Snatcher.* Four Winds, 1980.

Baylor, Byrd. *The Desert Is Theirs.* Scribner, 1975.

Baylor, Byrd. *Hawk, I'm Your Brother.* Scribner, 1976.

Baylor, Byrd. *The Way to Start a Day.* Scribner, 1978.

Caudill, Rebecca. *A Pocketful of Cricket.* Holt, 1964.

Crews, Donald. *Freight Train.* Greenwillow, 1978.

Crews, Donald. *Truck.* Greenwillow, 1980.

de Paola, Tomie. *Strega Nona.* Prentice-Hall, 1975.

Ets, Marie Hall. *Just Me.* Viking, 1965.

Feelings, Muriel. *Jambo Means Hello: Swahili Alphabet Book.* Dial, 1974.

Goffstein, M. B. *Fish for Supper.* Dial, 1976.

Goudey, Alice. *The Day We Saw the Sun Come Up.* Scribner, 1961.

Hodges, Margaret. *The Wave.* Houghton Mifflin, 1964.

Hogrogian, Nonny. *The Contest.* Greenwillow, 1976.

Hyman, Trina Schart. *Little Red Riding Hood* (by the Brothers Grimm). Holiday, 1983.

Isadora, Rachel. *Ben's Trumpet.* Greenwillow, 1979.

Jeffers, Susan. *Three Jovial Huntsmen: A Mother Goose Rhyme.* Bradbury, 1973.

Lionni, Leo. *Alexander and the Wind-up Mouse.* Pantheon, 1969.

Lionni, Leo. *Inch by Inch.* Astor-Honor, 1962.

Lionni, Leo. *Swimmy.* Pantheon, 1963.

Lobel, Arnold. *Frog and Toad Are Friends.* Harper, 1970.

Lobel, Arnold. *On Market Street*. Greenwillow, 1981.

Low, Joseph. *Mice Twice*. Atheneum, 1980.

McDermott, Beverly. *The Golem: A Jewish Legend*. Lippincott, 1975.

Musgrove, Margaret. *Ashanti to Zulu: African Traditions*. Dial, 1976.

Ness, Evaline. *Tom Tit Tot*. Scribner, 1965.

Plume, Ilse. *The Bremen Town Musicians*. Doubleday, 1980.

Preston, Edna. *Pop Corn and Ma Goodness*. Viking, 1969.

Ryan, Cheli. *Hildilid's Night*. Macmillan, 1971.

Rylant, Cynthia. *When I Was Young in the Mountains*. Dutton, 1982.

Scheer, Julian. *Rain Makes Applesauce*. Holiday, 1964.

Schweitzer, Byrd Baylor. *When Clay Sings*. Scribner, 1972.

Sendak, Maurice. *In the Night Kitchen*. Harper, 1970.

Sendak, Maurice. *Outside Over There*. Harper, 1981.

Shulevitz, Uri. *The Treasure*. Farrar, Straus & Giroux, 1979.

Sleator, William. *The Angry Moon*. Little, Brown, 1981.

Steig, William. *The Amazing Bone*. Farrar, Straus & Giroux, 1976.

Steptoe, John. *The Story of Jumping Mouse*. Lothrop, 1984.

Tafuri, Nancy. *Have You Seen My Duckling?* Greenwillow, 1984.

Tresselt, Alvin. *Hide and Seek Fog*. Lothrop, 1965.

Turkle, Brinton, *Thy Friend, Obadiah*. Viking, 1969.

Udry, Janice. *The Moon Jumpers*. Harper, 1959.

Van Allsburg, Chris. *The Garden of Abdul Gasazi*. Houghton Mifflin, 1979.

Willard, Nancy. *A Visit to William Blake's Inn*. Harcourt, 1981.

Williams, Vera. *Chair for My Mother*. Greenwillow, 1982.

Zemach, Harve. *The Judge: An Untrue Tale*. Farrar, Straus & Giroux, 1969.

Zemach, Margot. *It Could Always Be Worse: A Yiddish Folk Tale*. Farrar, Straus & Giroux, 1977.